BIRDS OF THE HAWAIIAN ISLANDS

BEING A

COMPLETE LIST

OF THE

Birds of the Hawaiian Possessions

WITH NOTES ON THEIR HABITS

BY

H. W. HENSHAW.

HONOLULU, H. T.

THOS. G. THRUM, Publisher.

1902

Lancer reprint edition, 2005

Originally published by
Thrum, Honolulu, 1902

New Material ©2005 by Lancer

Printed in the United States of America

ISBN: 0-935856-15-3 (Softbound Edition)
ISBN: 0-935856-16-1 (Hardbound Edition)

Lancer
PO Box 1188
Mount Ida, AR 71957
USA

INTRODUCTION.

Of recent years the study of nature has become popular and widespread in America. Not only is Nature Study taught in many of the schools, but the publications relating thereto have become very numerous. Unfortunately these various treatises apply wholly or in large part to the birds, insects, animals and plants of the mainland, few or none of which are found in the Hawaiian Islands. Such publications are hence of comparatively little use to island teachers and pupils or to the Islanders generally.

There being at present no popular work upon Hawaiian birds, the present little volume has been prepared with the view of breaking ground in this department, and with the hope that it may prove of assistance to those who are already bird-lovers and, as well, may stimulate others to become such.

For superbly illustrated volumes upon Hawaiian birds the reader is referred to the fine works issued by Mr. Walter Rothschild and by Mr. Scott B. Wilson.

Since the first part of the present treatise was published, the Bishop Museum has issued a "Key to the Birds of the Hawaiian Group" by W. A. Bryan. This valuable work supplies a ready means for the identification of all the birds thus far found upon the islands, and should prove a welcome and efficient aid to a knowledge of the subject. Much of the preliminary field-work in relation to the island plants, insects, shells and fishes has already been done by private investigators or by public institutions, and the results have been published. (Note the extensive and valuable memoirs on various branches of biology issued conjointly by the Royal Society of London, British Association for the Advancement of Science and the Bishop Museum under title of "Fauna Hawaiiaensis"). Investigations of a similar character are now being carried on by our own Government and by the Bishop Museum.

The description of new species and general field investigations are but the preliminary work which must precede publication in the form of popular treatises, and it is to be hoped that such may be issued on all the various departments of island biology as well, as upon its ethnolgy and archaeology.

Much as has been done in the past in island biology, vastly more remains to be accomplished in the future, and the study of island natural history will offer an attractive field for investigation and for discovery for many years to come. The work is vast, the laborers few, and it is to be hoped that the scientific interest and value of this work may appeal to those who are island born not less than to students from abroad.

The Hawaiian Islands, more remote from the continents than any others, have developed fauna and flora peculiar to themselves, and though the broad principles of biology apply here as well as elsewhere, the specific facts are different and possess a significance of their own which is yet to be fully interpreted. The forms that have been developed here, not only of birds but of plants, insects and mollusca, are very extraordinary and interesting, and the manner of their evolution and the causes leading thereto offer an inviting field of research hardly to be equalled elsewhere.

Hitherto little or no interest has been manifested by Hawaiians themselves in the subject of Hawaiian birds, and perhaps chiefly because of such indifference the needed protective legislation has not been enacted for the benefit of the latter. Even the inadequate protection intended by present statutory law has not been secured to them, since the laws have not been generally enforced and have been practically disregarded.

The remoteness of the forest which Hawaiian birds inhabit and the extreme dislike of the latter for any innovating changes such as attend civilization are doubtless chiefly responsible for the general ignorance respecting the very existence of most of the native birds, to say nothing of their songs and habits. Unlike many European and American birds, which flourish in the garden and orchard and find comfort and safety in man's protection, none of the island species seem to desire to be on neighborly terms with man, or to be capable of adapting themselves to the changes which follow in his wake. For a time they are content to fly over his clearings and to feed in the forest hard by; but to nest by his door and profit by his bounty seem to be foreign to their wild natures and presently, unable to reconcile themselves to his unwarranted intrusion into their ancient fastnesses, they retreat to the unvexed and virgin forest.

That certain Hawaiian birds are dying out there is only too much reason to believe, but the necessity for the preservation of large forest tracts for the retention and preservation of rain has recently become so manifest that effective legislation in this direction is sure to follow soon, with the important secondary effort of affording safe shelter for the birds. The preservation of the forest in large tracts will in all probability insure the perpetuity of a greater or less number of species of the latter; so that opportunity will be afforded for an acquaintance with and a study of the birds for an indefinite number of years to come.

BIRDS

OF THE

Hawaiian Possessions

WITH NOTES ON THEIR HABITS.

PART I.—SCOPE OF THE PRESENT LIST.

With the exception of a limited knowledge of Oahu and a short visit to the slopes of Haleakala on Maui, the author's own field experience is restricted to the Island of Hawaii, the largest and most extensively forested of the group, and mostly to its windward side. Within this limited area he has enjoyed unusual opportunities to observe the habits of certain species.

Many of the birds that inhabit the Island of Hawaii recur upon the other islands. While the change of food and climate, in other words, of environment, has been sufficient to transform many of them into specifically distinct forms, yet the habits of the related forms usually differ but little on the several islands and the songs still less. Hence, observations of habits made upon one island in the main apply to the allied birds of the other islands. In the case of species which have not fallen under the observation of the author, he has been aided by the published accounts of Wilson, Rothschild and Perkins.

It has been thought desirable to describe every species occurring on the islands. Sometimes the descriptions are brief, but it is believed that in all cases they will suffice for the identification of the birds. Those who may desire fuller descriptions are referred to the works of Rothschild and Wilson, or to the Key to Hawaiian Birds recently issued by the Bishop Museum. The descriptive material in the two former works has been freely drawn upon by the author in the case of many species not contained in his own collection. In the case of American species occurring in Hawaii, similar aid has been derived from Ridgway's excellent "Manual of North American Birds."

HAWAII AS AN ORNITHOLOGICAL FIELD.

Owing chiefly to their isolation, there are few land areas in the world possessed of greater interest for the ornithologist than the Hawaiian Islands, and, until recently, there were few of which the avian inhabitants were so little known. Of late years, chiefly owing to the labors of English ornithologists, our knowledge of Hawaiian birds has greatly increased. Many new species have been discovered by Wilson, Palmer and Perkins, and so thoroughly have the investigations of these naturalists been conducted that we may feel sure that the number of endemic land birds now known to inhabit the islands will never be materially increased.

The insular waters, however, have received comparatively little attention, and it is probable that a few species of water-birds remain to be added to the list, even if no new species are discovered.

There is no doubt, too, that the present list of Hawaiian birds will be materially increased by additional records of American species. There are certain birds, like the golden plover, turnstone, wandering tatler, bristle-thighed curlew and shoveller duck, which annually winter in the islands, and the habit is of long standing. As successive flocks of these birds leave the American coast for Hawaii, a greater or less number of individuals belonging to species of kindred habits mingle with the adventurous travelers, and by them are led to the unknown (to them) tropic islands. Every season some of these strangers visit these shores, but the number of observers is so small that, for the most part, the visitors escape detection. Examples of this class are the black-bellied plover, sanderling, red phalarope, red-breasted merganser and red-backed sandpiper, most of which are recorded for the first time as Hawaiian birds in this list.

Some of these species, like the sanderling, are probably even now forming the habit of annual migration to the islands, while others are to be regarded, so far as our present knowledge goes, as purely casual visitors.

The writer feels sure that the list of these stragglers will continually increase, as observers multiply, until it includes practically all the American west coast migratory species that are sufficiently strong of wing to endure the protracted and laborious flight over the ocean.

OBSTACLES TO ORNITHOLOGICAL STUDIES IN HAWAIIAN ISLANDS.

Prior to the investigations of the above-named naturalists, next to nothing was known of the habits of Hawaiian birds. Their labors, particularly those of Mr. Perkins, have done much to enlighten us upon this subject. The difficulties, however, in this branch of the study, though not insuperable, are very great. So that, notwithstanding the important contributions of the English naturalists, there is still offered an inviting field for future study and investigation.

The chief obstacles in the way of field studies in the islands are the dense forest, the steep mountain ridges beset with dense vegetation, and the extreme rainfall. The woods are so dense that progress in them is all but impossible except by cutting trails, and, as the tangled growth restricts vision upon all sides, birds are very difficult to watch and keep in sight. In this respect, however, a new era is dawning, at least upon the Island of Hawaii. Good roads and passable trails not only permit, but invite, the steps of the nature-lover into the heart of the forest which before was a terra incognita to all but the most hardy and the most enthusiastic. Opportunities to study Hawaiian birds are thus offered not only to the professional ornithologist, but to every nature-lover as well. The field is so broad and even, yet so little worked, that the intelligent observer cannot fail to discover facts of interest to himself and of positive value to science.

Of the nests and eggs of Hawaiian birds we know next to nothing. In fact it may be said that of only one bird, the *Elepaio,* have we an adequate knowledge of its life history, and even this statement must be qualified by adding that even of it there remains much to be learned.

DESTRUCTION OF HAWAIIAN FORESTS.

While the forest recesses upon the Island of Hawaii are being rendered more accessible all the time, it is not to be overlooked that the forest upon this and the other islands is being rapidly destroyed. Large areas are now falling before the axe preparatory to cultivation, and the birds that once inhabited them are being hemmed into tracts of constantly diminishing size, even if the birds themselves are not destroyed with the forests.

The deforestation of Hawaii is much accelerated by the work of cattle, which are ever increasing in numbers under the constantly increasing demand for beef. They browse upon the tender shrubs, vines and undergrowth, thus not only destroying the young trees and preventing their natural increase, but robbing the large forest trees of their natural protection. The trunks, accustomed to a heavy covering of mosses, lichens, ferns and vines, by which they are protected from the sun and wind and are ever kept moist, succumb to the new conditions, when the sun and wind have free access to them, and sooner or later die. Thus ohias, koas and other large forest trees are destroyed by cattle, though actually untouched by them.

Another source of danger to the forests is a span-worm, which has been identified by Mr. Perkins as the *Scotorhythra idolias,* which has done great damage to the koa of Maui and is now engaged in the same destructive work in Hawaii. Twice the present year (1901) the koa woods of Kaiwiki have been stipped by the larvae of this little moth, which exists in great numbers wherever the koa grows, and occasionally increase to countless myriads, when it stips every koa tree in its district.

This wholesale destruction of forest will soon materially diminish the number of Hawaiian birds—nay, already has done so—and in a few years the opportunity to study the habits of some of the unique bird forms which have been developed upon these islands will be lost forever.

ENVIROMENTAL CHANGES DISASTROUS TO HAWAIIAN BIRDS.

In connection with the disappearance of Hawaiian birds in past times, it should not be forgotten that, like all insular forms of life among which competition is slight or altogether wanting, they suffer much from slight adverse conditions, and even become extinct when the causes seem wholly inadequate. In the Island of Hawaii, the thinning out of a forest tract, nay, the cutting down of a certain portion on the edges of a large forest, is almost sure to be followed, sooner or later, by the almost complete abandonment of the tract by all its avian inhabitants. So, too, the making of a road through a forest, with the limited passing traffic, seems to have a disturbing influence upon Hawaiian birds absurdly out of proportion to the cause.

The author has lived in Hawaii only six years, but within this time large areas of forest, which are yet scarcely touched by the axe save on the edges and except for a few trails, have become almost absolute solitude. One may spend hours in them and not hear the note of a single native bird. Yet a few years ago these same areas were abundantly supplied with native birds, and the notes of the oo, amakihi, iiwi, akakani, omao, elepaio and others might have been heard on all sides. The ohia blossoms as freely as it used to and secretes abundant nectar for the iiwi, akakani and amakihi. The ieie still fruits, and offers its crimson spike of seeds, as of old, to the ou. So far as human eye can see, their old home offers to the birds practically all that it used to, but the birds themselves are no longer there.

It is more reasonable to conclude that the former inhabitants of such tracts have abandoned them for the more profound solitudes higher up than that they have perished from such slight causes. However, even the abandonment of forest tracts under such circumstances seems inexplicable, and the writer can recall no similar phenomenon among American birds.

It cannot be doubted that the crowding together of the native birds, as the direct effect of deforestation, will sooner or later have a disastrous effect upon their welfare and numbers. As the forest diminishes the food supply of the birds (insects, berries and nectar) will diminish with it, and in time prove inadequate to the demand.

It is evident to all who have considered the subject that one or more conditions of existence in the past have proved unfavorable to the increase and spread of certain Hawaiian birds, and have caused the extinction of others. The necessity of continuous inbreeding has been suggested as adequate to explain the apparent inability of certain species to hold their own in the struggle for existence, and, in the absence of other and more tangible causes, certain facts relative thereto may be presented.

It is apparent that the birds that are least numerous and that live in much restricted habitats are the ones most subject to inbreeding. Of such island species, *Viridonia* offers, perhaps, the most marked instance, since it is confined to an area of but a few square miles in extent, within which narrow belt of woodland the bird is by no means common.

In such a case it would appear by no means improbable that inbreeding has been a potent factor in the failure of the bird to become numerous, and to extend its range into neighboring districts, especially when to all appearances the latter are precisely similar as regards their avian attractions and resources.

It would appear that forms like *Viridonia* differentiated from the parent stock and succeeded in maintaining themselves up to a certain point and for a certain time, and then either remained stationary, in respect of numbers, or entered upon a retrograde movement, tending perhaps, to ultimate extinction.

No doubt there are many cases where it would be difficult to determine whether a given rare and local form is at the beginning of development or nearing the end of its career; but not so in cases like *Viridonia*. A bird so very different from its allies can hardly be held to be at the commencement of its existence as a separate race, but, on the contrary, must be held to have reached its present stage of distinctness only after a very long period of time. It would seem to be much more probable that a bird so completely differentiated, if weak in numbers and occupying but a small area, is nearing the final stages of its career than that the species is in its incipiency.

The rarity and extreme degree of localization of such birds as *Viridonia* are the more remarkable and the more difficult to explain, unless upon some such theory as inbreeding, inasmuch as the environment of the bird up to within two or three years (its home is now being invaded by the axe) appears to have been peculiarly favorable, and is evidently markedly so for other *Drepanine* forms, such as *Heterorhynchus, Chlorodrepanis, Oreomyza* and *Loxops*, as is evidenced by their numbers.

In respect to its small numbers and the limited extent of country occupied, *Viridonia* is, perhaps, an extreme case among Hawaiian birds, but there are others scarcely less remarkable. *Pseudonestor* and *Palmeria* of Maui, and *Chloridops* and *Rhodacanthis* of Hawaii are closely parallel, though not so extreme, cases. These birds, except *Palmeria,* which occurs also on Molokai, are confined to single islands and to a comparatively small part thereof.

If inbreeding be accepted as a true and sufficient cause of the present insecure footing of *Viridonia* under environmental conditions of its own choosing, the same theory seems applicable in the case of the other species.

To the same list may also be added the extinct, or nearly extinct, *Ciridops*, and the extinct *Meliphagine* form *Chætoptila.* None of the above birds appear to have suffered from enforced conditions or external agencies, except as regards compulsory inbreeding.

The two latter species, indeed, were both extinct, or practically so, long before their forest haunts had been interfered with by man in the slightest degree. Whether or not inbreeding played any part in the tragedy, their extinction must, at any rate, be assumed to be due to what may be termed natural causes, since neither bird appears to have ever been the object of pursuit by the natives.

All the above birds differ so much *inter se* as to be separable generically, and must have started upon their independent paths ages ago. Like *Viridonia,* they are more likely to be nearing the close of their respective careers than to be just entering upon them.

If in the past, when their forest homes were untouched, island birds have suffered from the disastrous effects of inbreeding, how much more marked is likely to be its effect as the available habitat of the birds is more and more restricted by deforestation.

In this connection it is to be remarked that the species that rove most widely and are most widely distributed in each island and over the islands generally are, with one exception, the ones that are the most numerous and that appear to be the most hardy. In the consideration of such facts it is always easy to confound cause and effect, but here it is clear, at least, that these species are the ones that are least subjected to the penalties of inbreeding, be those penalties what they may. Their roving habits, even though these are by no means so marked as in the birds of other lands, afford opportunity for the mating of birds reared at a distance from each other, even though upon the same island, and under somewhat different conditions of food and climate.

Still more important to the birds of this class is the possibility of the infusion of fresh blood from the other islands. No one who has studied the habits of the island birds can doubt that the passage of individuals from one island to another is very infrequent. Still, such instances must occasionally occur, and doubtless tend to strengthen and invigorate the avian stocks concerned.

Such species as the iiwi, akakani, amakihi and ou are the best examples of the birds of this class, and they doubtless will survive so long as any forests remain. The three former move about to some extent with the change of the seasons, but more in pursuit of the flowering trees. The ou seeks the fruit of the ieie vine wherever he can find it.

That at least one of these species possesses unusual powers of adaptation to new and strange conditions is attested by the fact that the akakani, in somewhat changed form (*Himatione freethii*), exists upon the rather inhospitable island of Laysan. This island is some 600 miles to the northwest of the main group, and the transferrance of the bird thither was, no doubt, due to accident, as a heavy wind storm. In Laysan its environment is markedly different from that which surrounded it on the islands of the main chain. Yet the bird, though said to be the rarest of the Laysan land birds, exists in some numbers and seems to thrive fairly well, despite the necessity of continuous inbreeding. The entire lack of competition may, however, make partial amends for this disadvantage.

The several species of o-o, living and extinct, and probably also the extinct mamo, are to be classed with the above species having comparatively wide range, and there is no reason to believe that these latter birds would not still abound in the Hawaiian forests if they had not been pursued to the death for the sake of their feathers.

In connection with the probable future of Hawaiian birds, and aside from the question of inbreeding, it may be added that as new and less favorable conditions prevail, the more highly specialized forms will naturally be the ones to suffer first and most, since they will be the least able to adapt themselves to changes, more particularly those involving the food supply.

The probable extinction of the koa forests, for example, at no distant day is likely to be followed, even if all other conditions should remain unchanged, by the extinction of such birds as *Pseudonestor* and *Rhodacanthis,* because of the extreme dependence of these species for food upon this tree.

Such birds as *Chasiempis,* the several forms of *Chlorodrepanis* and *Phæornis* are much more likely to survive new conditions indefinitely, if for no other reason than that less specialized habits endow them with larger resources in the way of food and also with greater adaptability. Even the honey-eaters, the most prominent of which are the iiwi and akakani, will long survive, since they are to no small extent insectivorous already, and could doubtless become exclusively so without injury. In a sharp struggle for existence, their chance for survival as against some of the more specialized forms would be excellent.

At least one Hawaiian bird is intensely local in disposition, but, despite its fondness for one locality, it has become very numerous, and is widely dispersed on several islands. This is the omao (*Phæornis*). This bird has adopted food habits which have subjected it to little or no competition. A confirmed berry-eater, it finds food everywhere abundant in the dense forest and in great variety.

If, as the result of localization, inbreeding produces any ill effects upon the vitality of *Phæornis,* they would seem to be more than counterbalanced by abundant food and the absence of competition. It is to be remarked, however, as having an evident bearing upon its probable future fate, that *Phæornis* declines to live in any but dense and undisturbed forest tracts, and many years ago became extinct upon the island of Oahu.

Allusion has been made above to the possibility of an interchange of avian strains by the passage of birds from one island to the other, and a few words on the subject may be added.

It is a surprising and remarkable fact that channels varying from only ten to thirty miles in width should prove all but impassible barriers even to small birds, to say nothing of those the size and stength of a large hawk. It is at once evident that if such channels actually prove barriers to the passage of birds, the cause lies in the disposition of the birds and not in the physical obstacles.

That these narrow inter-island channels have not always proved impassible to birds is conclusively shown by the fact that several of the genera are represented on all the islands of the main group by the same species (*Vestiaria* and *Himatione*), and that several others are represented by such nearly related species that the latter could have originated only from a common stock.

Having once entered and become established on an island,

however, the several species have readily adapted themselves
to the new conditions which, though apparently differing but
slightly, have yet proved sufficiently distinct to impress a number of the birds with new and, in some cases, markedly different
specific or varietal characters.

The intense spirit of localization which restrains birds within
the limits of a single island resulted, no doubt, primarily from
the absence of competition. Hawaii, Maui, Lanai, Molokai and
Oahu under ordinary conditions are each visible in turn from
the other, and the short distance and prevailing calm weather
would seem to invite the birds to inter-island visits. No doubt
anything like severe competition would compel them to longer
or shorter excursions to other islands, and thus, among other
effects, would tend to break down the extreme specific and generic
differences which now prevail and which make the islands so
interesting an ornithological field.

FAUNAL ZONES.

The Hawaiian Islands are practically nothing but vast accre-
tions of lava-mountain masses, sloping on all sides more or less
abruptly to the encircling sea. Authorities are agreed that the
islands increase in age from east to west, Kauai thus being the
oldest island and Hawaii the youngest. The latter, with its
three great mountain masses, has but one or two extensive
basin-like valleys, practically the only level land of much extent
being the Kohala plains. Both Oahu and Kauai contain valleys
of size, and, between the two lava mountains of Maui, is a broad
and level connecting isthmus. Molokai also has valleys of considerable proportions.

As, however, the valleys have long been forestless, and probably never were forested in their lower extensions, the consideration of faunal belts is practically limited to the mountain slopes.

The author's own investigations are limited chiefly to the island
of Hawaii. which is not only more extensively forested than
any of the others but the forests, up to comparatively recent
times, have been but little disturbed. The following remarks
will be understood, then, as applying more particularly to that

island. Nevertheless, the main geographical relations of the fauna and the flora appear to be much the same upon all the islands, though each island, no doubt, presents peculiarities due to local conditions.

Present available data are all too insufficient for an accurate definition of the ornithological life zones of the islands. Indeed, owing to the general climatal sameness and the similarity of the forest belts and the consequent wide range of the birds, it may be doubted if such life zones can ever be defined with the precision attained elsewhere. A consideration of the subject, however, discloses some interesting facts which may here be briefly set forth

LOWLAND ZONE.—Hillebrand (Flora of the Hawaiian Islands) found it possible to differentiate more or less sharply four zones according to the plant life. Of these, three only have much interest for the ornithologist.

His first or lowland zone has but slight interest in the present connection. It is the open country, grass-covered, with scattered clumps of trees (chiefly ohia) and extending to a variable but always slight elevation above the sea. The rainfall in this belt is considerable, probably nowhere falling below 100 inches per annum, while the average temperature ranges between 70 and 80 degrees Farenheit.

Except casually and in small numbers, it is not probable that this lower belt was ever occupied by any of the passerine species. It probably always was, as it is to-day (save for the introduced mynah and rice birds) almost an avian desert, uninhabited because no passerine birds adapted, or capable of adapting themselves to such conditions ever chanced to find their way to the islands. It may be remarked in passing that the short-eared owl abounds in this zone, but extends its range into the next one.

This belt of comparatively open country offers excellent opportunities for the introduction from America of ground-loving species friendly to agricultural interests, although it cannot be overlooked that all ground-building species must now contend for existence against a formidable foe in the shape of the mongoose. Yet the experiment upon a liberal scale is well worth trial.

LOWER FOREST ZONE.—This zone may be defined as extending from about 500 feet to 1,500. It is well marked by its vegetable productions, especially by the kukui (*Aleurites moluccana*), lauhala (*Pandanus odoratissimus*), and by the hau (*Paritium tiliaceum*), which do not pass beyond it, as also by the awapuhi (*Zinziber zerumpet*), the ti (*Cordyline terminalis*) and the ohia ai (*Eugenia malaccensis*). The ieie (*Freycinetia arborea*), important as furnishing the chief food of the ou, abounds, but extends into the next zone. The ohia (*Metrosideros polymorpha*) constitutes the bulk of the forest in this, as in the next zone, but does not attain the proportions and vigorous growth characteristic of the tree higher up. The same is true of the koa, which makes its appearance here.

There are no birds that are characteristic of this zone. *Chasiempis, Phæornis, Chlorodrepanis, Psittacirostra, Himatione, Vestiaria* and *Buteo* are all present, in small numbers towards its lower edge (or altogether wanting), but in increasing numbers towards its upper confines.

There is evidence tending to show that the above species formerly extended somewhat lower down than they do now, and in greater numbers, especially *Chasiempis*. In the past fifty years the treeless area has been constantly creeping upwards as the direct result of deforestation by the planter and indirectly by the work of cattle, elsewhere alluded to, and this has considerably affected the range of the birds.

The temperature is somewhat cooler than in the preceding zone and the rainfall also is greater.

MIDDLE FOREST ZONE.—The middle forest region may be defined as extending from about 1,500 feet to 6,000 feet. This region is within the belt of greatest rainfall (130-180 inches), and upon all the islands is by far the richest botanically, and in all forms of animal life, including the birds.

The temperature varies much between the upper and the lower confines, but the average summer temperature is not above 65 degrees and in winter falls considerably below that. At 6,000 feet altitude, or a little above, frosts are not unknown in summer and are of common occurrence in winter.

The prevailing forest trees are first the ohia; second the koa (*Acacia koa*), both trees being of prime importance in the domestic economy of island bird life. Both furnish food, shelter and nesting sites to the greater number of island passerine birds. Both trees extend above and below this zone, but here they attain their greatest size and development. It is the home of all the *Rutaceae* and most of the *Araliaceae*. Here are the alani, the olapa, the kawau and many other berry-bearing trees and shrubs. In this belt the ferns flourish in wildest luxuriance, and the giant tree ferns attain their greatest size and abundance. Here occur on all sides the tree lobelias, those remarkable endemic plant forms, of interest to the ornithologist as furnishing more or less nectar to several species of birds.

In addition to the birds enumerated as living in the next lower belt and extending their range into the present one, several species are present in this zone that descend below only casually. Here belongs, or did belong, the extinct mamo; and here today are found *Moho, Hemignathus, Heterorhynchus, Oreomyza, Loxops, Chloridops, Pseudonestor, Palmeria, Ciridops, Loxioides,* and *Rhodacanthis*. It is highly probable that it was in this belt that *Chœtoptila* lived its allotted span of life, though our knowledge of the former haunts of this extinct species is too scanty for definite statement.

Upper Forest Zone.—The upper forest zone of Hillebrand extends from about 6,000 feet to 8,000 or 9,000 feet, and is characterized, according to that author, by stunted mamani (*Sophora chrysophylla*), *Cyatheoides,* the naeo (*Myoporum*), and others. Here luxuriate shrubby *Compositae, Raillardiae, Dubautia, Campylotheca* and *Artemisia*. Here grow wild strawberries and ohelos (*Vaccinium*) which also abound in the barren lava tracts of the middle belt.

The chief interest this belt has for the ornithologist arises from the fact that it offers a home most of the year to the Hawaiian goose, which also inhabits the lava flows of the middle zone, and in summer temporarily visits the lowland belt for nesting purposes.

This upper zone is inhabited scantily, if at all, by forest birds, and then only on its lower edge, which is perhaps occasionally visited by the finch-like forms *Chloridops* and *Pseudonestor,* as also by the honey-eating species when the trees of the middle region have ceased flowering.

It is doubtless neither the altitude nor the cool climate of this upper zone that repels the birds, but the fact that above about 6,000 feet the large forest trees rapidly dwindle to scrubby and depauperate forms that possesses no attractions for the birds, since they afford neither shelter nor abundant insect or other food.

Between the upper limits of this zone and 11,000 feet, where Hillebrand fixes the limit of vegetation on Mauna Kea, the vegetation grows ever scantier and scantier till there is little else but bare lava rocks.

DISEASES OF HAWAIIAN BIRDS.

I am not aware that the birds of the Hawaiian Islands are more subject to fatal diseases than those of other lands. Dead birds are, however, found rather frequently in the woods on the island of Hawaii, especially the iiwi and akakani.

There is no doubt that sudden and marked changes of temperature affect Hawaiian birds unfavorably, especially the two species just mentioned and, after heavy and prolonged storms, many individuals of both species are driven into sheltered valleys and even along the sea-shore far from their woodland haunts. Under such circumstances scores of the above named species are picked up dead or dying, and the mortality among other birds is, perhaps, unusually great.

Every naturalist who has visited the islands has noticed the presence of certain tumors or swellings on the feet of the birds. The tumors are mostly, perhaps wholly, confined to the woodland birds. The writer has found them upon the feet of the iiwi, akakani, omao, elepaio, amakihi, *Oreomyza* and the genera *Hemignathus* and *Heterorhynchus.* They have not been present on any of the many specimens of hawks he has examined, but Mr. W. Newell tells me that he has seen hawks thus affected.

There are certain localities, as in Olaa, where in some seasons a considerable percentage of the birds collected show unmistakeable tokens of this disease, past or present.

Sometimes the tumors are as large as peas, and it would seem that their presence must seriously incommode the bird's movements if nothing more. Evidence, however, is not wanting to show that frequently such tumors have serious consequences. The writer has seen a number of birds that had lost one and even two toes from one foot, and he remembers one specimen in which the ankle joint was so much involved that it seemed probable that the whole foot would eventually have sloughed off. Often, however, the tumors slough away with little or no damage, save to leave the integument rough and thickened.

Nor are the tumors confined exclusively to the feet of birds, for several have been shot which had large tumors around the rictus of the bill.

Dr. Nicholas Russel, of Olaa, has kindly examined under the microscope slides made from two specimens, and he pronounces the tumors to be of undoubted bacillic origin.

There is little doubt that the bacilli are derived from the wet bark of trees. All the birds affected with the disease, which I have thus far examined, have come from the windward side of Hawaii, where the annual rainfall is from 130 to 180 inches. Upon this theory of origin it is easy to understand how the bacilli occasionally infect the region of the mouth since the bird frequently may be seen rubbing the bill and side of the mouth against the branches to clean them; and again in scratching the throat and head the bacilli may readily be conveyed from the claws.

ORIGIN OF HAWAIIAN BIRDS.

There is no more interesting question concerning Hawaiian birds than that relating to their origin. With the exception of a few species that are evidently comparatively recent comers from America, like the night heron, gallinule, marsh hawk and the short-eared owl, Hawaiian birds are quite unlike any others.

They fall naturally into a few groups of related species, and so different are they from the birds of other lands that their relationships are traceable only with great difficulty. Nor can all the questions involved in the problem be considered settled.

Much valuable light has been thrown upon the subject by Dr. Gadow, who has studied the anatomy of many of the species with interesting and valuable results. These are set forth at length in an Appendix to Wilson's Birds of the Hawaiian Islands, to which the reader is referred.

Dr. Gadow's general conclusions may be summed up as follows: The bulk of the birds that are distinctively Hawaiian belong to a family to be called the *Drepanididæ*, which, with little doubt, are of American origin. They appear to be nearest related to the present American family of the *Cærebidæ*. The *Drepanididæ* were probably the first avian inhabitants of the islands, and have been here a very long time, as is evidenced by the remarkable changes they have undergone and by the numerous related species they have differentiated into.

Later a second infusion of avian stocks occurred, this time from the continent of Australia, of which the elepaio and the several species of o-o are living examples, and the *Chaetoptila* an extinct one.

ORNITHOLOGICAL KNOWLEDGE OF HAWAIIAN NATIVES.

The impression seems to be general that in olden times the natives were extensively acquainted with Hawaiian birds, which is true, and that even the present day natives are very well posted on the subject; the latter is by no means the case.

We may gain some idea of the extent of the bird lore of the natives by their methods of naming and classifying the birds. Wherever it was possible the native name for a bird is imitative of its note or cry, and the Hawaiians, aided no doubt by their flexible, vocalic language, appear to have been very skillful in coining these imitative names. Elepaio, io, uuau, aukuu and many other bird names might be cited as evidence of this initative faculty. By means of the proper accent and pitch such words may be made to give an almost exact idea of the bird's call.

Of nice scientific discriminations of form and structure the natives knew little and cared less and, according to modern ideas, their classification was decidedly crude.

The birds that found place in their myths and legends, like the elepaio and pueo, and those that were important in their domestic economy, like the duck and plover, which they ate, and the mamo, oo and iiwi, whose feathers were valued for decoration, they naturally knew well and had distinctive names for. Indeed for some species, like the iiwi, they had several names, the precise meaning and application of which we do not now know. They even called the iiwi in its first or speckled plumage iiwi popolo, though they must have been well aware of its relationship to the adult bird.

Closely allied species, as we now know them to be, they frequently called by the same name, either not noting the difference or, as is perhaps more likely, not thinking the differences important enough to be worth naming. The several species of amakihi are examples. Soo, too, upon the island of Hawaii, amakihi is applied to both the *Chlorodrepanis virens* and the *Oreomyza mana.*

A few birds appear to have been so rare and so local that they were quite unknown to the natives; at all events they seem not to have been named by them. The *Viridonia,* which is confined to a very small area of dense forest on either side of the Wailuku river, Hawaii, is a conspicuous example of this kind. The writer has shown skins of this bird to a number of natives reputed to be well acquainted with Hawaiian birds—one of whom was born within Viridonia's territory—but none of them had ever seen it alive or could give it a name. One of the old men, indeed, maintained its identity with the amakihi, although it is nearly twice the size of that bird and by no means of the same color.

But in ancient times, no doubt, as above stated, the knowledge of birds was far more widely spread among the Hawaiians and more accurate than it is today. Indeed the younger generation are almost absolutely ignorant even of the names of the birds, and are quite ignorant of their habits.

In the olden days when it was an important part of their duty for the priests to watch the motions of certain birds and listen to their songs that by this means they might learn the will of the Gods, and when the bird-catcher plied his calling that the feather tribute might not be wanting to pay the taxes imposed by the chiefs, then we may be sure bird-lore was well-nigh universal.

The bird-catchers, especially, must have been thoroughly familiar not only with the haunts of all the feathered kind, but with their songs and their habits.

But taxes are no longer payable in feathers; no longer does the bird-catcher ply his calling; the priest no more reads auguries from the songs of birds; the old days have gone forever, and with the old days and the old conditions have gone the greater part of Hawaiian bird-lore.

HISTORY OF ORNITHOLOGICAL INVESTIGATIONS IN THE ISLANDS.

The history of ornithological investigations in the Islands is on the whole a brief one, and a few words devoted to the subject may be of interest. An admirable resume of the subject by Prof. Alfred Newton was published in Nature for 1892 and is quoted in the introduction to Wilson's Birds of the Hawaiian Islands above referred to, from which the following notes are chiefly culled.

As is well known the Islands were discovered by Cook in 1779. The natural history specimens obtained by Cook came from the islands of Kauai, Niihau and Hawaii. The first knowledge of the Islands' avian inhabitants based upon the Cook collections, reached the world in 1781-85 through Lathams' General Synopsis of Birds. Most of the actual specimens collected by Cook's ships, probably not very many in number, have been lost. The loss is the more unfortunate as Latham's original descriptions, as well as Gmelin's, which were based upon those of the former, leave much to be desired, both in respect to precision and sufficiency. Moreover the early collectors took little pains in labelling specimens, and either did not label them at all or indicated their source as "Sandwich Islands," leaving the particular island to be guessed; for the great differences now known to exist between the birds of the several islands, were not suspected

by the early investigators. It seems probable that the Island of
Hawaii supplied the larger number of specimens to Cook's collectors, but in the case of any given species there can be no cer-
tainty. Owing chiefly to this doubt as to the exact point of
origin, some of the species described by Gmelin have proved
stumbling blocks to ornithologists ever since the descriptions appeared.

The quarter of a century that followed the discovery of the
Islands is a blank, so far as their ornithological history is concerned; they were frequently visited by ships but not by naturalists.

In 1816-17 Chamisso and Eschscholtz accompanied Kotzebue
in his visit to the islands, but these naturalists seem to have paid
no attention whatever to the island birds.

In 1824 H. M. S. "Blonde" visited the islands having on board
Mr. Andrew Bloxam, "who was something of a naturalist," and
it was intended that the published account of the voyage should
contain a proper appendix on the natural history of the islands.
Of the natural history report of this voyage Mr. Newton says:
"An appendix there indeed is, but one utterly unworthy of its
reputed author, for the book was edited by a lady who had nothing but a few of his notes to guide her, and though assisted, as it
is stated, by 'the gentleman connected with that department in
the British Museum' the Appendix is a disgrace to all concerned,
since, so far from advancing the knowledge of the subject, it introduced so much confusion as to mislead many subsequent
writers."

Having had access to the original notes of Mr. Bloxam, Mr.
Wilson is able to supplement the meager contents of the Appendix with the statement that the bird collection contained "twenty-
five specimens of land birds—one of them bearing the M. S. name
of Turdus Woahensis." Thus we learn the interesting fact that
the Island of Oahu once possessed a form of the Hawaiian Thrush
(*Phæornis*) long since extinct.

The Blonde bird collection has shared the fate of so many of
the early collections, and no discoverable trace of it remains.

In 1835 the American naturalist, Townsend, and the equally

well known naturalist, Nuttall, visited the Islands of Oahu and Kauai of the group, and spent three months. At the end of the year Townsend returned and, with Deppe, the Prussian naturalist, spent some time in natural history pursuits, visiting most of the windward islands before finally leaving, which he did in March, 1837.

Our gain in knowledge of the avifauna of the islands resulting from the visits of these three investigators was comparatively little. Nothing was published by the investigators themselves though their collections contained several new species of birds. Nuttall was an exceedingly good observer, and notes from him on the habits, and especially upon the songs, which he had a happy knack of describing, of any of the birds he must have seen upon Oahu and Kauai would have been of great value. Again anything like a thorough collection of the birds then existing upon the islands would now be of inestimable worth since it must have contained representatives of certain species, not only now extinct but of which not a single specimen is in existence.

One of Townsend's observations made in the Island of Kauai is so interesting, referring as it does to a long forgotten practice of the natives, that I cannot refrain from quoting it here entire from Wilson's Introduction:

"We made here several long excursions over the hills and through the deep valleys, without much success. The birds are the same as those we found and collected at Oahu, but are not so numerous. They are principally creepers (*Certhia*) and honey-suckers (*Nectarinia*); feed chiefly upon flowers, and the sweet juice of the banana, and some species are very abundant. The native boys here have adopted a singular mode of catching the honey-sucking birds. They lay themselves flat upon their backs upon the ground, and cover their whole bodies with bushes, and the campanulate flowers of which the birds are in search. One of these flowers is then held by the lower portion of the tube between the fingers and the thumb; the little bird inserts his long, curved bill to the base of the flower, when it is immediately seized by the fingers of the boy, and the little flutterer disappears beneath the mass of bushes. In this way dozens of beautiful birds are taken, and they are brought to us living and uninjured."

Much of ornithological interest was to have been expected from the Wilkes' expedition of the year 1840 from the zeal and ability of its well known naturalists, Pickering and Peale. During their six months' stay considerable collections were made, but nearly all of them were lost in the wreck of one of the ships, the Peacock. Of the original report upon the mammals and birds by Peale, nearly all the copies were destroyed by fire, a new edition being brought forth by Cassin in 1858.

In 1852 Fr. Hartlaub published an extract of the results of the Wilkes' expedition, and in his summary of the birds inhabiting the islands he includes thirty species, though two of them are marked as doubtful. Commenting upon Hartlaub's list, Prof. Newton remarks that "one of them is now known to be rightly included, but the other must be struck out, as well as, for one reason or another, four more—leaving a total of twenty-five, only sixteen of which are land-birds and only fourteen passeres."

So stood our knowledge of Hawaiian birds till 1869 when a "Synopsis of the Birds hitherto described from the Hawaiian Islands" was communicated to the Boston Society of Natural History by Mr. Sanford B. Dole, and was published in the proceedings of the Society for that year. This list proved a notable advance on our previous knowledge, and included 48 species, the author stating his belief that this number "probably comprises but little more than half the avifauna of the group"—a very accurate estimate as it proved. A revision of this list, in which some of its errors were corrected, appeared in the Hawaiian Annual for 1879.

About the year 1887 Mr. Valdemar Knudsen made many valuable and interesting collections of natural history upon the island of Kauai, and much of his material was sent to the National Museum. The birds were studied by Dr. Stejneger, and the results were published in the proceedings of that institution for 1887. By Mr. Knudsen's efforts several new species of birds were discovered, all of them on the island of Kauai.

The year 1887 marked a new era in the history of Hawaiian

ornithology, since that year witnessed the inception of the labors of Mr. Wilson, an enterprising young Englishman, whose work in the Islands, completed in 1890, was crowned with most gratifying success. His collection of island birds was the most extensive made up to that time, containing no fewer than fourteen new species of Passeres, including two new genera. In addition Mr. Wilson was able to place in the hands of Dr. Gadow specimens of the most important avian types still existing in the islands, and this material formed the basis of most important conclusions as regards the systematic position of Hawaiian birds and of their derivation. The beautifully illustrated quarto which embodied the results of Mr. Wilson's labors, published in parts, was issued in complete form in 1899.

The years of 1890-92 were years of renewed activity in the study of Hawaiian birds. Two collectors were sent to the islands by Mr. Rothschild, and very large and important collections were made by them. These collections were sent to the Tring Museum, England, and formed the basis of many important contributions by Mr. Rothschild to English scientific journals and later of the royal quarto entitled "The Avifauna of Laysan and the Neighboring Islands, with a Complete History to date of the Birds of the Hawaiian Possessions." This volume, in three parts, with its many and fine illustrations, and including in its scope the whole Hawaiian group, must ever remain a landmark in Hawaiian ornithological literature.

The year 1892 also witnessed the beginning of the natural history work in the islands of Mr. R. C. L. Perkins. This gentleman was sent out conjointly by the British Association for the Advancement of Science and by the Royal Society. His general collections were very large, and are by far the most important ever made in the islands. They are deposited in the British Museum and in that of the Cambridge University, England. A considerable number also are in the Bishop Museum, Honolulu. Not the least important part of Mr. Perkin's contributions to the natural history of Hawaii are his notes upon the habits of its birds. Though not a professed ornithologist, Mr. Perkins published material showing him to be an acute and accurate observer, and his observations went far to fill the previous lacunae respecting this interesting subject.

Mr. Perkins' series of birds included almost all the rarer species still extant, and contained one new species. The fact that so keen an observer and so energetic a collector as Mr. Perkins was able to add but one new species to the list sufficiently attests the thoroughness with which Mr. Perkin's immediate predecessors performed their work.

For all practical purposes the list of island birds is to be regarded as complete. Yet the discovery and description of all the birds inhabiting the islands is to be looked upon but as the necessary preliminary to a still more important study, viz.: the life-histories of the birds, of their relations to each other and to the avi-fauna of other lands.

PART II.—DESCRIPTIVE.

TURDIDÆ.   THRUSH FAMILY.

Phæornis obscura (Gmelin).   Omao; Kamao.

The omao, which is the only Hawaiian representative of the Thrush Family, is found abundantly all over the island of Hawaii, but only in the denser forests above one thousand feet. The bird is so shy in some districts, as in parts of Olaa, that it is very difficult to catch sight of, and in consequence is wholly unknown to the settlers except by its voice, while in other localities, not far distant, its disposition is exactly the reverse, and the bird may often be seen, and its habits studied, at short range.

Wherever found, it is prodigal with its song and calls, and its notes do much to dispel the prevailing stillness of the Hawaiian forest. The song is jerky and consists of widely-spaced syllables, but is pleasing and, at times, sweet. The omao sings its sweeter strains while on the wing. In Spring, particularly, the bird seems to be unable to express its feelings from its wonted perch and, leaving the top of some tall tree, it circles widely about flooding the air with its notes. The omao is preeminently a berry-eater and, as it finds an abundance of berry-bearing shrubs growing far up on the stems of the lofty ohias as well as upon low trees, such as the kopiko, kawau, mamake and others, it rarely or never descends to the ground.

Though berries are its chief fare the year round, it does not wholly disdain insect food, and I have seen the omao hunting insects over the large limbs of the koa with considerable energy and celerity. Once or twice I have even seen the bird launching out after a flying insect, but in such clumsy fashion as to reveal a woeful want of practice in the business of fly-catching. It does not disdain spiders upon occasion, and in the stomach of one individual, I found a minute land-shell. In the breeding season I once found in the bill of a male several of the brown caterpillars which infest the koa and ohia trees, which the bird was probably carrying to its young. Nevertheless I wish to reiterate the statement that the omao is essentially a berry-eater and that insects form a rare and inconsiderable part of its fare. Of the many birds I have dissected the stomachs of not five per cent have contained insects, and then only in very small proportion. The stomachs of the vast majority have been crammed with berries and with berries only.

It is a common habit of the omao to alight on a limb lengthwise, a custom which, with its erect attitude while perching, strongly indicates thrush affinities.

All observers have noted the curious habit of the omao of shaking its wings as if in an ague fit. The wings are allowed to drop loosely by the sides, and are then shaken with a tremulous motion, precisely as young birds do when begging food from their parents. A succession of these fits always seizes the omao when an intruder is observed and, if the antic was reserved for such occasions only, it might be set down in so shy a recluse as nervous apprehension. But the writer has often observed the omao when himself unnoticed, and has seen the bird indulging in the luxury of a trembling fit all by himself. The habit is common to all the species of the genus, into the origin and meaning of which it is probably useless to inquire. It is worth remarking that the habit is not confined exclusively to omao but is shared by all the species of *Chasiempis.*

Abundant and widespread as is this thrush, practically nothing is known of its nesting habits. The author feels assured that the bird nests far up in the tall forest trees, and that only by the merest accident will its nest be found.

In March of 1899, while at Kaiwiki, I shot an adult io (*Buteo solitarius*) ; and upon dissecting it I found in its stomach a small fragment of egg-shell which I suspect was a portion of the egg of an omao. It was of a light blue color sprinkled with minute splashes of reddish brown. The size, as indicated by the fragment, would well correspond to a bird the size of omao and, at all events the egg both in size and color seemed to be essentially Turdine in character. The mynah, the nest of which io sometimes robs, as is well known, lays a blue, unspotted egg. This note is published for what it is worth and, unsatisfactory though it is as evidence, I believe it affords a hint of the character of the omao's egg.

Description.—Adult. Upper parts dull olive-brown, crown and forehead tinged with grey; beneath smoky-grey, fading into white on the abdomen; lower tail-coverts tinged with buff; flanks dull russet; rectrices dark brown, edged with russet; base of inner primaries and secondaries bright russet, forming a broad band. Legs light brown; soles greenish yellow; bill black; soft parts of mouth light yellow. Length about 6.75 inches.

Juv. plumage. Head above clove brown, with shaft-streaks of light buffy; back, edges of primaries and secondaries sepia, most of the feathers edged with blackish, and with arrow shaped shaft-streaks of buff; chin and throat light grey; belly, white; feathers of lower throat, breast and sides edged with black, and with triangular spots of light buff; under tail-coverts russet, flanks tinged with same. Length about 7 inches.

Phæornis oahuensis Wilson. Oahu Thrush.

Thanks to the diligent inquiry of Mr. Wilson we now know that the island of Oahu formerly possessed a member of this family of thrushes, and that in 1824 specimens of the bird were obtained on the island by Bloxam, the naturalist of the "Blonde," who gave it the manuscript name of *"Turdus woahensis"* (see Wilson Birds of the Hawaiian Islands p. XIII.)

The bird doubtless became extinct long ago, and its seems never to have been seen, or at least recorded, from Bloxam's day to this.

The manuscript description is as follows: "Length 7½ inch. Upper parts olive-brown, extremities of the feathers much lighter color; tail and wings brown; bill bristled at the base."

As Bloxam's manuscript contains a description of the thrush inhabiting the island of Hawaii (*P. obscura*) which he rightly considered a different species, we are safe in believing that the Oahu bird was fully entitled to a distinct name, although no specimens of the bird are now known to be in existence.

Phæornis myadestina Stejneger.   Kamao.

This is one of two representatives of the thrush family found upon Kauai. Palmer describes it as being " a quiet bird and not shy." Its song "reminded him of that of an English thrush, but it was less powerful, although it could be heard at a great distance," and in his opinion was sweeter.

Its habits and its food appear not to differ materially from those of its relative on Hawaii.

Description.—Adult. Entire upper surface of a dull hair-brown with an olive tinge; sides of head dull tawny, the feathers fringed with dusky; lower surface of a light smoky gray, light on throat and fading into nearly pure white on abdomen and under tail-coverts; breast and flanks olive-gray; base of inner primaries and secondaries bright russet. Three outer tail-feathers tipped with white which gradually shades into brown. Length about 8 inches.

Phæornis palmeri Rothschild.   Puaiohi.

This bird, the smallest island representative of the thrush family, inhabits Kauai where it was first obtained by the Rothschild collectors, though its presence in the island seems to have been known previously by Mr. Francis Gay and to the natives by whom it had received a distinctive name. Its habits and its song appear to differ considerably from those of the other species.

Description.—Adult. Above dull brown, with darker head and almost uniform wings and tail; inner web of external pair of feathers and center of next pair buff; a white orbital ring, beneath greyish, becoming nearly white on the abdomen and buff on the lower tail-coverts; a whitish patch on the under surface of the wing quills. Length about 6.75 inches.

Phæornis lanaiensis Wilson. Olomao.

This *Phæornis* is said by Wilson, who discovered and described it, to inhabit both Lanai and Molokai. I quote from Rothschild: "The olomao, as it is called, both on Lanai and Molokai, is not rare on both these islands, and Palmer saw it in the lowland as well as at the highest elevations. In the stomachs he found seeds and berries of different plants."

Description.—Adult. Much like the other species. May be distinguished from *obscura* by its smaller size and whiter under-parts; from *myadestina* by its smaller size and the absence of the white markings on the tail. Length about 7.50 inches.

SYLVIIDÆ. SYLVIA FAMILY.

Acrocephalus familaris (Rothschild). Miller Bird.

According to Rothschild this little bird is very abundant on the island of Laysan to which it is confined. It is an energetic insect eater, searching for its prey among the roots and grasses. It is especially fond of a large white moth abounding on Laysan and called "miller," whence the name of the bird. The bird nests in tussocks of grass, and lays three pale bluish eggs, blotched with olive brown.

Description.—Adult. Upper parts greyish brown. Below buffy white. Length about 4½ inches.

MUSCICAPIDÆ. FLYCATCHER FAMILY.

Chasiempis sandwichensis (Gmelin). Elepaio.

The elepaio is one of the most abundant of all Hawaiian birds, and it is one of the most beautiful and interesting. In some districts it descends almost to sea-level, but it is most numerous at a middle altitude, say from 1,000 to 3,000 feet. The bird is

3-H B

equally at home in the tops of the tallest trees and in the lowest shrubbery and, occasionally, it descends even to the ground in search of insects. Perhaps if it has a favorite hunting-ground next to the ohia tree, it is the mamake, because that tree, with its abundant berries, harbors many insects, and no clump of mamake is without a pair of these little birds.

The curiosity of the elepaio is insatiable and a pair or two are always on hand to inspect an intruder and to learn his business. It will follow and catch an insect on the wing which it has chanced to dislodge from some hiding place, but it never sits and watches for flying insects as do the American flycatchers. In fact by far the greater parts of its insect food is gleaned from the branches of trees and shrubs, and from among the lichens and tangled ferns. Its motions generally and its hunting habits are those of a wren rather than those of a flycatcher. Indeed its resemblance to the wrens is remarkable, especially when it droops its wings by its side and cocks its tail over its back, which is its frequent habit.

Elepaio appears to be the only Hawaiian woodland bird that nests low down habitually. I once found a nest of this bird on the horizontal scape of a fern (*Sadleria*) within two feet of the ground.

This, however, is a very exceptional location. Usually the nests are situated in a small tree in the shade of the forest, like the mamake, young koa, or one of the berry-bearing trees, like the kawau, and are placed from ten to thirty feet up. The nest is built in an upright fork or saddled upon a horizontal branch and supported by lateral twigs, and is a beautiful structure, made of grasses woven into a deep cup and most tastefully decorated on the outside with fern fronds and lichens held in place by silk strands taken from spiders' webs.

The elepaio usually lays two eggs, sometimes three. They are of a pure grayish white, more or less profusely sprinkled with reddish-brown dots. No bird has a more important place in Hawaiian mythology than the elepaio, and omens and warnings were formerly read from its actions and notes. Of the latter it has several. Its name is the native interpretation of its song—if it can properly be called a song—and the bird iterates and re-iterates this all day long, so that no one with ears to hear need ever be in any doubt as to the identity of elepaio. It has, besides, several call-notes, one of which is a true flycatcher-like whit.

It is a most active little bird and is busy about something the day long, now engaged in searching every nook and crevice for insects, now chasing a comrade in play in and out of the leafy forest coverts.

Description.—Adult. Above rufous brown; upper tail-coverts white; forehead, lores and superciliary stripe white or (in most specimens from the windward side of island) chestnut; wing coverts white, spotted with black; feathers black at base, more or less white tipped, especially in females; sides of body and chest reddish brown; abdomen and under tail-coverts white; outer edge of outer tail feather mostly white; inner web white for nearly half its length. Length 5.50-5.75.

Juv. plumage. Above ochraceous brown; upper tail-coverts ochraceous; wing-coverts brown tipped with ochraceous; under parts brown and buffy; abdomen greyish white.

Chasiempis gayi Wilson. Oahu Elepaio.

This is the elepaio of Oahu and is one of the commonest, if not the commonest, of all the small native birds left on the island. This is what might be expected from its habits, and it is probable that when most of the Hawaiian birds are extinct the elepaio will long continue to maintain itself in scarcely diminished numbers. So long as any woodland at all is left elepaio will hold its own.

Description.—Adult. Above brown, slightly tinged with tawny ochraceous buff; forehead, ear-coverts and an ill-defined line above the eye ochraceous buff; rump and upper tail-coverts white; quills deep brown narrowly edged with pale brown on the outer webs and broadly edged with white inwardly. Rectrices blackish brown, largely tipped with white. Feathers of the chin, throat, and upper breast black more or less tipped with white. Abdomen and under tail-coverts white; breast and sides of body washed with brown. Length about 5.50 inches.

Juv. plumage. Above tawny ochraceous brown, bright tawny ochraceous on the upper tail-coverts. (Rothsch.).

Chasiempis schlateri Ridgway. Kauai Elepaio.

Three only of the islands are favored by the presence of a species of this genus. Molokai and Maui for some reason, are both lacking the bird. The habits of the three species do not differ essentially.

Description.—Adult. Above dark smoky grey with a brownish tinge; forehead and space around the eye washed with pale buff; rump and upper tail-coverts white. Quills blackish brown, margined with pale brownish ash on the outer webs, and with white on the inner webs; secondaries white tipped. Tail blackish brown; outer tail feathers tipped with white. Wing-coverts, except the primary, tipped with white below whitish, strongly tinged with brownish buff on the throat, breast, and sides of the body, darkest on the breast. Under tail-coverts and axillaries white. Length about 5.59 inches. (Rothsch.).

CORVIDÆ. CROW FAMILY.

Corvus tropicus Gmelin. Hawaiian Crow. Alala.

The Hawaiian crow is a singularly local species, and it may be doubted if in the whole world there is another crow the habitat of which is similarly restricted. Though called the Kona Crow, the alala is numerous in the forests of both the Kona and Kau districts of Hawaii, outside of which island it has never been found. The bird ranges also into the scanty woods on the lava along the Kau road below the Volcano House, and Mr. Oliver Shipman informs me that a few pairs used to breed in the koa forest some two miles west of the Volcano House. This locality brings the bird within sight of the Hilo district, into which the bird seems not to desire, or perhaps to be able, to pass. As food suitable for the crow abounds in the Olaa woods, the only apparent cause for the bird not spreading further northward would seem to be the more abundant rainfall on the windward side of Hawaii.

The alala, like its congeners, seems to be almost omnivorous and like them it possesses the unfortunate habit of robbing the nests of other birds, even taking the eggs and the young of the mynah.

The alala has quite a variety of odd notes but includes in its repertoire a ringing caw, caw, which sufficiently betrays its relationship though the note is pitched upon a much higher key than that of our old friend, "Jim Crow" of America.

It would be difficult to imagine a bird differing more in disposition from the common American crow that the Hawaiian alala. The bird, instead of being wary and shy, seems to have not the slightest fear of man, and when it espies an intruder in the woods is more likely than not to fly to meet him and greet his presence with a few loud caws. He will even follow the stranger's steps through the woods, taking short flights from tree to tree, the better to observe him and gain an idea of his character and purpose.

The alala is as impudent as he is curious and noisy, and will invade the chicken yard daily to share with the fowls their food, when it requires something more than moral suasion to induce him to leave.

The nest of the alala is much like the ordinary structure of the crow elsewhere, and is made of coarse sticks with a lining of finer material. It is placed in an ohia or similar tree, not necessarily high up, and the eggs are laid in the early summer months. I am not aware that the eggs have been described.

Description.—Adult. Dusky brown throughout, head and tail blacker. Feathers of chin and upper throat bristly, with shining black shafts. Primaries, especially towards tip, lighter brown. Bill bluish black; legs and feet black. Total length about 19 inches; female smaller.

DREPANIDIDÆ. DREPANINE FAMILY.

Hemignathus obscurus (Gmelin). Hawaii Akialoa.

The akialoa is one of the most remarkable and interesting avian forms which has been developed upon the islands. The present species is limited to the island of Hawaii, but Oahu, Kauai and Lanai are, or formerly were, each represented by a species of akialoa. Why this bird has not made a home on the islands of Maui and Molokai it would be hard to say.

Upon Hawaii generally the akialoa must be considered as rare. The deep forests of Olaa would seem to be peculiarly fitted to its habits, but it was only after long search that the writer found the bird there at all and then only upon a few occasions. Whatever may have been the case formerly it is now rare there. It is more numerous in the still denser forest of koa and ohia north of the Wailuku river, though by no means common even there. It is probably more numerous in Kona.

The stout legs and sharp claws of this bird enable it to pass rapidly over the large limbs of koa and ohia, and to cling in any and to seize from their hiding places in the tangles of ferns and mosses various sorts of grubs, beetles and their larvae which are its chosen food. I have never seen the akialoa feeding upon the nectar of flowers though other observers have, but it is probably a rare habit.

The akialoa is especially fond of probing into the deep, cup-shaped leaf clusters of the ieie vine. These are usually full of dead leaves and fallen trash, in the recesses of which insects are perfectly safe from all birds except the akialoa and its relative, the akiapolaau, the latter being furnished with a similar hooked probe. I have no doubt that the peculiar leaf clusters of the ieie have had more to do with the development of the extraordinary bills of these two birds than anything else.

The akialoa has a characteristic call, but I have never heard it sing, though I have often met with the pairs in the breeding season.

Description.—Adult. Above bright oil-green; wing and tail quills dusky brown, margined with dull green; a well defined superciliary stripe of gamboge-yellow. Lores black. Beneath dull olive green; legs and feet plumbeus; bill bluish black, base plumbeus. Length about 6.5 inches.

Juv. Dull olive above, tinged with green; beneath olive-yellow; sides and flanks warm olive; superciliaries pale yellow.

Hemignathus procerus Cab. Iiwi.

This Kauai species is said to be known to the natives by the name iiwi. If so the transfer of names is somewhat surprising. The bill is even of more extraordinary proportions than that of the former species. Its chief food, no doubt, is insects, but, according to Mr. G. C. Munroe, it also sucks honey from the lehua flowers. This observer also reports that the species has a sweet song.

We learn from him further that "this bird is much more common and enjoys a wider range than the nukupuu, which bird it much resembles in habits. It seems to inhabit the whole forest region of Kauai."

Description.—Adult. Head above olive, feathers edged with olive-green, giving a spotted appearance; back, edges of wing and tail quills and of wing coverts bright olive-green; wing and tail quills ashy brown; a bright yellow superciliary line, and a black loral spot. Throat and breast deep olive-yellow, merging into sulphur-yellow on abdomen; tibiae dull white. Length about 7.50 inches.

Adult female. Above greyish olive; rump and upper tail-coverts olive green; a dusky loral spot below olive-yellow; sides and flanks olive-green.

Hemignathus lanaiensis Rothschild.

Several specimens of this species were obtained on Lanai in 1892 by Mr. Rothschild's collectors, but it is doubtful if the species is still in existence, as it was then very rare.

Description. Adult male. Differs from *H. obscurus,* its nearest ally, in its much longer and very stout bill, ashy-greyish tint of the crown, and much duller olivaceus green of the back, neck, and rump. Breast dirty yellow, gradually passing into dull olive on the flanks, instead of bright yellowish olive as in *H. obscurus.* Under tail-coverts creamy white, instead of olive-green. (Rothsch.)

Hemignathus ellisianus (Gray).

This form of the akialoa used to inhabit the forests of Oahu where Mr. Wilson thinks it may still linger in small numbers. No collector, however, has seen the bird for many years and its existence is open to much doubt. The single specimen in the Berlin Museum is supposed to be the only specimen extant.

Description.—Above greenish olive-brown, more greenish on the back and rump and more greyish on the head and hind-neck; the dark bases of the feathers on the head showing through. Lores deep brown. A distinct yellow superciliary stripe. Chin, throat, and middle of abdomen dull brownish white (apparently somewhat faded). Upper breast olive-greenish; sides of breast and flanks dull olive-greenish. More olive-brown on the flanks. Wings and tail deep brown, bordered with yellowish green. Under wing-coverts dull white. The bill is brown, somewhat horn-brown, but *not blackish* as in all the other species of *Hemignathus.* (Rothsch.).

Heterorhynchus wilsoni Rothschild. Akiapolaau.

In the akiapolaau we have another of the interesting and extraordinary bird forms with which Nature has favored the Hawaiian Islands, there being a distinctive species for each island. In external form this bird resembles the akialoa, though more compactly and robustly built than that bird, but the yellow belly and the short, blunt mandible, in contrast with the long, delicate maxilla, serve at once to distinguish the two apart. The differences of form, and especially the different bills, indicate a corresponding difference in habits, of which, indeed, these differences are the direct result.

The akiapolaau frequents the same deep forests as the akialoa, though by no means wholly unknown in more open woods, and like that species it passes over the large limbs and trunks of trees with great rapidity, all the while peering to the right and left for the hidden haunts of its insect food. It has the same habit of probing into the leafy crowns of the ieie vine and into the thick mosses and lichens. But the short, blunt mandible of the akiapolaau has conferred new powers upon it which the other bird does not possess. By means of it, when the maxilla is agape, it can flake off lichens and even pound off small knobs and excrescences under which it suspects larvae to be concealed. Again, fixing itself firmly to a limb by its stout claws, it will seize a small excrescence between the mandibles and tug away at it till it wrenches it off, when it probes the cavity beneath for larvae with its upper mandible. The skull is unusually thick, and the muscles of the neck and the maxilla are remarkably developed so as to permit this double function of the bill as a hammer and as a wrench. To some extent then the akiapolaau has progressed towards the structure and the functions of a woodpecker, though in the main it is very different from any of the members of that tribe, not a single representative of which has found its way to the islands.

It may be added in passing that no family of birds is more needed in the islands than the woodpeckers. Dead timber is very abundant in the forests and, as Hawaiian insects lead hidden lives for the most part, the woodpeckers would prove of immense service in tearing open their burrows and in reducing their numbers. Having to do without woodpeckers, however, Nature has attempted to accomplish their work in a very different way. She has endowed several birds with stout legs and sharp, strong claws to enable them to run swiftly over the trunks and limbs of trees. She has given to others long bills and brush tipped tongues for probing hidden cavities and seizing the insect prey; and she has equipped the akiapolaau with a special device in the shape of a more or less effective hammer to expose the hidden retreats of larvae.

But to return to our akiapolaau. So far as the general forest is concerned the bird is a rather rare one, but in certain localities north of the Wailuku I have found it rather common. It has a short but sweet warbling song which it utters at frequent intervals as it is engaged in hunting.

Description.—Adult male. Above bright olive-green, brighter on head and rump; wing and tail quills brown, edged with olive-green, as also the wing-coverts; a black loral spot; beneath gamboge yellow; sides and flanks washed with olive-green; legs plumbeus; bill bluish-black, bluish at base. Length about 5.75 inches.

Adult female. Above dull olive with faint greenish cast, greener on rump; beneath olive-yellow, much deeper on chin and throat, sides and flanks greenish-olive.

Young. Are much duller above than the female; below olive, washed with yellowish, especially on abdomen. Both the females and young differ much individually, as regards extent and depth of color.

Heterorhynchus lucidus Lichtenstein.

This is the Oahu representative of the akiapolaau. As suggested by Wilson, it is probable that the original specimens upon which the species rests were collected by Deppe and Townsend in Nuuanu Valley in 1837. The species has not been seen since by any explorer, and it is all but certain that it is extinct. Very few specimens exist in museums.

Description.—Adult male (in Paris Museum). Above olive-green, darker and more olive on the back, lighter and more green on the head, wing, and tail-coverts. Lores and a line behind the eye, brownish-black;

across the forehead a narrow, and above the eyes a conspicuous orange-yellow superciliary stripe. Quills deep brown, outer webs edged with greenish yellow. Chin, throat and upper breast bright orange-yellow; abdomen yellow. (Rothsch.).

Heterorhynchus affinis Rothschild.

Found only upon Maui where it is generally confined to the more elevated forest. Mr. Perkins states that this bird has two songs, one of which is identical with that of the Hawaii species, while the other is much like that of the house finch introduced from California. He finds that the food of the Maui species, like that of the form on the island of Hawaii, consists mainly of insects, "but the birds are quieter and less vigorous in their movements." He records the fact also that this species sucks honey.

Description.—Adult male. Top of head bright gamboge-yellow, passing into yellowish-green on the nape and hind neck, the green being rather abruptly terminated by the grayish olive-green of the back, brighter and greener on the upper tail-coverts. Quills and rectrices deep brown, bordered with bright olive green. Lores black, connected by a black band across the forehead. A tiny black chin spot. Throat bright yellow, passing into sulphur-yellow on the abdomen and pale yellow on the under tail-coverts. Sides of body tinged with greenish-olive. (Rothsch.). Female much duller.

Heterorhynchus hanapepe (Wilson). Nukupuu.

The nukupuu inhabits the forests of Kauai, from an elevation of from 2,000 to 3,000 feet, where it seems to be decidedly rare. Like its congeners, whose general habits it shares, the nukupuu lives chiefly upon insects. The fact that all of the several species of this curious genus live principally upon insects is attested by all who have observed their habits. Indeed the result of these observations might have been predicted from a study of the birds' structure. Long centuries of insect hunting, under the peculiar conditions found in the Hawaiian forest, have impressed upon the birds of this genus the stamp of extreme specialization. Their modification has been all in one direction, and their equipment is that of the highly specialized insect hunter.

Mr. Wilson was informed by natives that the nukupuu eats also bananas and oranges, an interesting fact if confirmed.

Description.—Colored much like others of the genus, especially the *H. wilsoni* of Hawaii, from which it is at once distinguished by the curved, instead of straight, under mandible. Length about 5.60 inches.

Viridonia sagittirostris Rothschild. Green Solitaire.

This beautiful bird was one of the most interesting discoveries made by Palmer, Mr. Rothschilds' collector, in the island of Hawaii where alone it is found. It is one of the rarest prizes among existing Hawaiian birds and its habitat is limited to the dense forest a few miles in extent upon either side of the Wailuku River, at an elevation of from 2,000 to 4,000 feet. Yet even in its stronghold one may watch for it for days in vain, unless he know its call note, when occasionally a pair may be called up out of the forest fastnesses. Having attracted its attention in this way I have succeeded on several occasions in luring one up to within a dozen feet, and have listened to its rather plaintive call note.

The long straight bill is oriole-like in character and, like the orioles, the *Viridonia* seems to live chiefly upon insects which it gleans from the foliage of the ohias, to which tree it seems to confine its attention chiefly. The bird seems to be wholly unknown to the natives and I have been unable to learn its native name, if indeed it ever had one. I have therefore ventured to call it as above.

Description. Adult. Above bright olive-green, brighter on head and rump; an inconspicuous dusky spot anterior to eye; below yellowish-green; wing dark brown, feathers edged with green; a tail of a lighter shade of brown, edged with green; under surface of wing dark ash color; elbow yellow; under wing-coverts light yellowish green; legs plumbeus; bill bluish-black, base of L. M. bluish. Length about 6.5. Female generally duller and smaller.

Chlorodrepanis virens (Gmelin). Hawaii Amakihi.

This little green and yellow bird is one of the commonest of the island species, and is very widely diffused. In this respect it differs markedly from many Hawaiian birds which inhabit only restricted areas specially suited to their habits.

The amakihi loves the nectar of flowers, and is frequently to be seen in company with the iiwi and the akakani rifling the ohia blossoms of their sweets. It has learned also that the imported nasturtium secretes a fine quality of honey and, however close to the house the flowers may grow, it pays them regular morning and evening visits. As the amakihi has a comparatively short bill it is quite unable to reach the nectar, deep down in the long spurred corolla, and, like the iiwi, it has learned to pierce the spur with its bill just over the nectaries, and in this way easily reaches the coveted sweets.

It is the amakihi also that pays so much attention to the banana blossoms, and daily visits them for the sake of the abundant nectar. This bird hunts, too, all over the broad leaves of the same plant for minute insects which no other bird does. But the amakihi spends most of its time hunting for insects in the foliage of the ohia trees and among the low shrubbery.

It is to be remarked that this species confines its search for insects almost entirely to the foliage, and spends very little time on the trunks and the larger branches. Exactly the reverse is true of the *Oreomyza,* which frequents the same localities, and rather closely resembles the amakihi in size and general appearance. Bearing this difference in habits in mind, the two species may almost always be distinguished at any distance.

The call note of this species is a low sweet "tweet" which is frequently uttered. Its song is a low, simple but, withal, a rather sweet trill which is repeated at rather frequent intervals.

The nest of this species seems to be placed at various heights in the ohia and other trees. It is composed of roots and bark, lined with rootlets. The eggs I have not seen.

Description.—Adult male. Above oil green; beneath greenish-yellow; lores black; wing and tail brownish, edged with green; lining to wing whitish. Bill about .65 long; slightly curved; grayish plumbeus; legs plumbeus. Length about 4.50 inches. Female similar but duller.

Chlorodrepanis wilsoni Rothschild.   Maui Amakihi.

Under the above name Mr. Rothschild has separated the Maui amakihi, considering that it has a larger bill than *virens* of Hawaii on the one hand, and is somewhat differently colored from *chloris* of Oahu on the other, a view apparently accepted by Mr. Wilson. The writer also is inclined to consider this view correct, though his present material is only sufficient to show that the Maui bird is remarkably like *virens*. Though the bill of Maui specimens appears to average larger than that of *virens,* yet I suspect that individuals may occur which it will be impossible to determine without knowing the island whence derived. In the juvenile plumage Maui birds seem to be much greyer than the similar stage of *virens* from Olaa. I have not compared skins from Maui with the Oahu bird.

Mr. Rothschild, with material before him from Molokai and Lanai, declines to admit the validity of Wilson's *Chlor. kalaana and chloridoides,* a view which I shall accept for the present.

I found *wilsoni* to be rare in June on the slopes of Haleakala above 5,000 feet, but to be commoner below that elevation. Its habits and notes seem to be much like those of *virens* of Hawaii. The old birds were leading about their families of young which were fully fledged.

Chlorodrepanis chloris (Cabanis).   Oahu Amakihi.

This is the Oahu amakihi. Probably its habits differ in no essential respects from those of its allies. According to Mr. Seale the bird is not rare on the timbered mountain ridges and in the gulches.

Description.—Adult male. Above bright yellowish-green, with black forehead and lores; wings and tail brownish-grey, edged with green; below golden yellow. Length 4.5 inches.

Chlorodrepanis stejnegeri (Wilson).   Stejneger's Amakihi.

This is one of two species found upon Kauai, both of which are known to the natives by the name of amakihi. This bird possesses a more robust form than any of its congeners and a

stouter and more curved bill. Its habits probably do not differ in
any essential respects from those of the species just described.

Description.—Adult male. Entire upper surface bright olive-green;
lores blackish; primaries, secondaries and tail smoky brown; throat,
breast and sides lemon yellow, passing into whitish on the belly and under
tail-coverts. Length about 4.40 inches; bill about .65; strongly curved.
Female similar but duller.

Chlorodrepanis parva (Stejneger). Alawi; Anauanii.

This species is an inhabitant only of the island of Kauai where
it was first obtained by Mr. Knudsen. According to Wilson it is
found throughout the forest region, and has been taken by Mr.
Francis Gay towards the summit of Waialeale (4,000 feet), the
highest point on the island.

I see no reason for the removal of this species from the genus
Chlorodrepanis. It is true that it has a nearly straight bill. It
must not be overlooked that the bills of the other members of the
Chlorodrepanis group differ considerably inter se (more especially
the bills of *stejnegeri* and *virens*) and, in respect of its curvature
of bill, *parva* seems to connect *Chlorodrepanis* with *Oreomyza*.
In its other features, however, *parva* seems to be strictly congen-
eric with *chloris, stejnegeri* and *virens*. The character of the
tongue alone is sufficient to show that it does not belong in
Oreomyza. *Parva* seems, indeed, to be closely related to *C. virens*,
from which it is chiefly to be distinguished by its smaller size and
its shorter and straighter bill.

Description.—Adult. Entire upper surface and sides of body as well as
the outer edges of quills and tail feathers bright yellowish olive-green,
inclining to olive-yellow on the forehead, region above the lores, super-
cilia, and rump; trace of a dusky line between bill and eye; under surface,
including under tail-coverts, bright olive yellow; middle of abdomen,
tibiae, axillaries, and under-wing coverts white, except those of the latter
nearest to the edge of the wing, which are bright yellow; quills blackish,
edged in the outer web with yellowish olive, in the inner one with white.
Length about 4.30. (Stejneger.)

Oreomyza mana (Wilson). Olive-green Creeper.

This little olive-green bird in certain districts of Hawaii is common, and in others rare. Throughout the Olaa woods, for instance, even at an elevation at from 2,000 to 3,000 feet, the species is rare, but in the forests of mixed koa and ohia along the Wailuku river it is numerous. The bird is common also in the koa woods above the volcano. It appears not to be found at all at low elevations, but occurs from about 2,000 feet upwards.

So nearly of a size are the amakihi and this species, and from a distance so nearly alike in color, that by the novice they may be easily mistaken one for the other. In habits, however, they are quite unlike. Whereas the amakihi, as above stated, hunts for insects among the foliage and the smaller twigs, the present species creeps along the trunks and the larger branches, gleaning from the interstices of the bark and from the mosses and lichens its insect fare. Its food consists very largely of the larvae of beetles, which its sharp, straight bill enables it to procure with ease, provided they are not deeply hidden. In respect to its food and its general habits, the olive-green creeper may well be compared with the akialoa. Both birds frequent the same localities, live upon much the same food, and procure it in much the same way, save that the much longer bill of the akialoa enables it to explore depths for the hidden larvae which the other cannot reach. So far as I am aware the *Oreomyza* never touches honey.

Description.—Adult. Upper parts dull green, brighter on rump; feathers of head with dusky centers giving a slightly mottled appearance. Under parts greenish buff, shading into yellow on abdomen and into whitish on chin and throat. Wings and tail blackish brown, margined with green. Lores and space beneath eye black, in some specimens tending to orbital ring. Legs brown; Maxilla dark brown; lower mandible light brown; length about 4.50.

Specimens in the juv. plumage have the abdomen cream color, the chin and throat almost white, with a superciliary line of white which, in one specimen, extends clear across the forehead. In very young birds the lower mandible is yellow.

Oreomyza perkinsi Rothschild. Perkins' Creeper.

Concerning this newly described species I quote as follows from Rothschild: "This remarkable specimen has a long but straight bill; the nostrils are covered by an operculum, which, however, leaves a minute space at the lower margin open; the second primary is about one-tenth of an inch shorter than the third; the third, fourth, and fifth are nearly equal, but the fourth is a trifle longer. The coloration is that of *Chlorodrepanis virens.* The bird thus occupies a somewhat intermediate position between *Oreomyza* and *Chlorodrepanis,* and it might be a hybrid between *Oromyza mana* and *Chlorodrepanis virens;* but, as *Oreomyza parva* of Kauai occupies a similarly intermediate position between the genera *Oreomyza* and *Chlorodrepanis,* I think it is quite possible that it is a good species, and I have much pleasure in naming it after Mr. Perkins, who has done such very good work on the Hawaiian Islands in furthering our knowledge of their biology."

"Adult male. Above light olive-green (Ridgway, Nom. Colours, pl. x., No. 18). brighter on the rump. Quills black, edged with oil-green; tail-feathers dark brown, edged with oil-green. Below olive-yellow; vent greenish white. Thighs dirty white. Under wing-coverts white, with a yellow tinge; lores black. Iris dark brown. Legs and feet greyish brown. Soles of feet yellowish flesh-colour. Upper mandible dark brown, with paler base; lower mandible grey. Total length about 5.5 inches, wing 2.6, tail 1.7, tarsus 0.85, culmen 0.63.

One male, Puulehua, [Kona] Hawaii, September 25, 1891.

Resting as it does upon a single specimen, the status of this recently described species can hardly be considered as settled until after further investigation. Its description indicates that it is very closely related to the *Chlorodrepanis virens;* or, as suggested by Mr. Rothschild, it may be a hybrid.

Oreomyza bairdi Stejneger. Akikiki.

This is the Kauai representative of the genus. It is a larger, more robust bird than the one just mentioned and is differently colored, but in general habits the two species appear to resemble each other closely.

Description.—Adult. Above hair brown, tinged with pale green on rump and on margins of wing and tail feathers. Below olive-buff, nearly white on chin and throat, and tinged with pale yellow on the breast and abdomen. Lores whitish. Length about 4.45.

Oreomyza flammea Wilson. Kakawahie.

This beautiful species, the native name of which signifies "fire-wood," probably from its bright flame color, is found only upon the island of Molokai where probably it is not uncommon. Very little is known of its habits, but they probably do not differ essentially from those of its congeners.

Description.—Adult male. Front and sides of the head pure scarlet; top of the head and back brownish scarlet, brightening into nearly pure scarlet on the rump; chin, throat, and lower surface generally pure scarlet, but paler in hue, brightening, however, on the flanks; remiges and rectrices blackish brown, edged with brownish scarlet; wing lining pale scarlet.

Adult female. Top of the head hair-brown, but each feather brownish-scarlet at the base, and the shafts of those towards the back of the head grey; back hair-brown tinged with red; rump distinctly russet; upper tail-coverts brownish scarlet; remiges and rectrices blackish brown edged with brownish scarlet, as also are the upper wing-coverts. Beneath, dull white tinged with pale scarlet; sides of the body reddish brown, and wing-lining white tinged with scarlet. Length about 5 inches. (Wilson.)

Oreomyza newtoni (Rothschild).

I found this species to be very common in the woods of Haleakala at an elevation of between 4,000 and 5,000 feet; in fact it is the most abundant of Maui birds in the vicinity of Olinda.

When referring to the Hawaiian member of this genus (*mana*) I laid special stress upon its habit of hunting almost exclusively along the main stems of the trees and upon the large limbs, a habit which will almost invariably serve to identify the bird in the forests of Hawaii. The Maui species is noticeable for the same habit, but, unlike *mana,* it much frequents also the undergrowth, and not rarely descends even to the ground in its hunting excursions.

Such marked difference in habits between species so closely allied is extremely interesting, and I attribute it to the absence in Maui of the elepaio. The absence of the latter bird from this island is of itself remarkable, since in Hawaii, just across the channel from Maui, in plain sight and distant not more than twenty miles, the elepaio is very numerous indeed. The elepaio is essen-

4-H B

tially a bird of the low undergrowth, though by no means exclusively confined to it. As the undergrowth in Maui in unoccupied by any bird, *Oreomyza* has changed its habits and extended its hunting grounds, being indeed far more an inhabitant of the scrub than of the trees. In other words its habits are far less specialized in Maui than are those of its relative upon Hawaii where competition is keener.

Upon a few occasions I saw this species feeding upon nectar from the ohias, but this I believe must be considered a rare habit, as Mr. Perkins, who noted the same habit, also concludes.

In June the old birds were everywhere leading about young, and were feeding them principally upon the small green caterpillars of the koa and ohia.

The call note is quite unlike that of *mana,* being very similar to the chirp of our familiar song sparrow. Only once did I hear anything resembling a song from this bird. Then I was close to several younglings whom I was watching when a male flew almost to my feet and, after a chorus of excited chirps and pleading notes, burst into an ecstatic warbling song. It may be doubted if this outpouring is the regular song of the species, as it was quite unlike the voice of any other Hawaiian bird known to me. It was a melody born of extreme agitation and of the alternate emotions of hope and fear. If intended, as no doubt it was, to divert my attention and to secure immunity for its young it was a most touching and effective device.

Oreomyza maculata (Cabanis). Oahu Creeper.

This is the Oahu creeper. According to Wilson, this species is fairly common in the district of Halemanu where there are still some remains of the former forest. Palmer found it not rare in the upland districts of Waialua from 1,500 feet upwards. Perkins found it also at Kaiwaloa.

Description.—Adult male. Forehead, superciliary stripe, chin, cheeks, ear-coverts, throat, and breast golden yellow; rest of upper parts olive-green. Wing and tail feathers blackish brown, with olive-green edges, loral spot dusky. Beneath yellow, more whitish on the middle of the lower abdomen; sides of breast and flanks washed with olive-green. Under wing-coverts whitish, washed with olive yellow. Length about 5 inches.

Female very different from the male. Forehead, superciliary stripe and under parts yellowish white; sides of breast and flanks washed with olive-grey. Above olive, the greater wing-coverts with large greenish-white tips. (Rothsch.).

Oreomyza montana (Wilson). Alauhiio.

According to Rothschild, Palmer found this species on the southwest side of Lanai from about 1,500 feet to the highest peaks. It is not perhaps so very rare, though difficult to procure on account of the dense brush.

Description.—Adult male. Forehead, line above the eyes, and cheeks bright lemon-yellow; rest of upper parts light yellowish green, more greenish yellow on the rump and upper tail-coverts; margins of quills and recticles like the back. Beneath bright lemon-yellow; thighs brownish buff. Length about 5 inches. Female more greenish and duller.

Drepanis pacifica (Gmelin). Mamo.

There is every reason to believe that this famous bird is extinct, or so nearly so as to leave little hope that it will ever again be seen by human eyes. Nevertheless the writer saw at least a pair, possibly a whole family, in the woods of Kaumana, July, 1898. A year later I was assured by a native who had just come down from the deep forest, not far from the above locality, that a few days previously he had heard the note of a mamo near by but did not see it. His efforts to secure the bird, if he found any as he promised, were not successful. This fact brings the living history of the bird down to the year 1899.

The explanation of the extinction of this fine bird is doubtless to be found in the persecution it suffered at the hands of the natives, both in ancient and in modern times. Its feathers were more highly prized than those of any other bird, and were dedicated solely to the service of the higher chiefs. It may be doubted if the mamo was ever very abundant, nor is it likely that many of the feather mantles, even in ancient times, were made solely of the yellow feathers of the mamo. The bird was probably never numerous enough to permit of this extravagance. Still there is indubitable proof that a few such cloaks existed, and it is entirely

credible that their manufacture occupied several generations, and
that they were of priceless value when once made. The word
mamo had several meanings according to Andrew's Dictionary,
and one of them signified a yellow war-cloak covered with the
yellow feathers of the mamo. Alaneo was another name for a
royal robe made of the feathers of the mamo only.

It is said that the birdcatchers in Kamehameha's time, and perhaps before, were strictly enjoined not to kill any of the royal
birds, but to turn their captives loose when stripped of the coveted
yellow feathers. Had this injunction been strictly obeyed, the
golden harvest might have been reaped indefinitely without in any
wise affecting the welfare of the bird. But the forests in which
the bird-catcher plied his calling was distant and deep, and it is
possible that the injunction was not strictly heeded; for meat of
any kind was always scarce in Hawaii and in any form was highly
prized. However, the mamo was ever a wary bird and difficult
to secure, and we may feel tolerably sure that the ancient system
of the natives of limeing the mamo would never have caused the
bird's extinction, even if the kapu against its use for food was not
strictly observed. After the introduction of fire-arms into the
islands and they became at all general, bird lime rapidly gave way
to the quicker and more deadly shot-gun and the birds quickly
met their doom. In later historic times, at least, the mamo has
always been very rare.

We know next to nothing of the habits of the mamo. The
birds I saw in Kaumana were very active, and evidently were in
pursuit of insects which they were hunting in the very tops of the
tall ohias. The birds' flight from tree to tree was not rapid, but
was smooth and well sustained, and the bird on the wing reminded
me of nothing so much as the cuckoo. Though I observed the
birds at intervals for more than two hours, I did not hear a single
note.

Description.—Glossy black, with the exception of the lower part of the
body, the rump, the tail coverts both above and below, the feathers of the
tibia and those of the anterior margin of the wing, which are of a fine
crocus yellow; the larger primary wing-coverts and under wing-coverts
white, the former mottled with blackish grey, and the latter tinged with
yellow. Remiges brownish black, tipped with dull white on the external

vane of the five outer primaries, and both vanes of the next four, as well as those proceeding from the olecranon. Four middle rectrices glossy black, the rest more or less brown, and showing a patch of dull white near the tip, which though indistinct on the inner feathers becomes very distinct on the extreme pair. Bill and legs apparently deep brown. Total length about 8 inches. (Wilson.)

Drepanis funerea A. Newton. Black Mamo.

This species was discovered by Mr. Perkins upon the island of Molokai, to which island it is confined. He obtained several specimens at an altitude of about 5,000 feet. It appears to be rather closely related to the mamo and is somewhat smaller.

Description. Black throughout, except the outer edges of the primaries which are grey. Bill long and very much decurved; upper mandible much longer than the lower. Length about 8 inches.

Vestiaria coccinea (Forster). Iiwi.

This is one of the few birds which is generally distributed throughout the islands and, except at low altitudes, it is everywhere numerous.

The most highly colored of all Hawaiian birds, the iiwi, is also one of the most interesting. The disconnected notes of its rather sweet song may be heard coming all day long from the tall ohias when in blossom.

The iiwi is exceedingly fond of nectar, which is obtains chiefly from the blossoms of the ohia, but the bird does not disdain to rifle it from other flowers, both wild and cultivated. Nasturtiums and canna are especial favorites with it, and any one who is fortunate enough to live where the bird is common may attract numbers close to the house by planting the above named flowers. The birds will soon learn to visit the flower beds daily, especially in early morning and at eventide. Unable to reach the nectaries from the mouth of the nasturtium flower, even with their long bills, the iiwi has learned to pierce the spur of the blossom just above the coveted honey, and the brush tipped tongue enables them to scoop out the sweet drops and leave not a trace behind.

The iiwi is at all seasons also an energetic insect hunter,

though more particularly when nectar is scarce, and its crop is often crammed with a small green worm which infests the koa, the ohia, and other trees. The iiwi was the species chiefly depended upon in the olden times to furnish the red feathers for the cloaks and helmets of the lesser chiefs. Like the mamo, the oo and other bright feather-bearing birds, the iiwi was caught chiefly by means of bird-lime.

The flight of the iiwi, and also of the akakani, is accompanied by rythmic pulsations, which are audible at quite a distance, and which always betray the passage of the birds above the tree tops. The flight of no other Hawaiian birds are thus marked. I have fancied that the wing-beats of the akakani are pitched on a higher key than of the iiwi, and that the flight of the two are thus distinguishable.

Description.—Adult. General color bright vermillion. Wing and tail black; innermost secondaries white or white edged; under wing coverts white. Bill and feet vermilion; bill an inch long and much curved. Length about 5¾ inches.

Young in juvenile plumage (iiwi popolo) greenish yellow, variously mottled with black.

Palmeria dolei (Wilson). Crested Honey Eater.

This remarkable and interesting species inhabits the higher wooded districts of the island of Maui, to which island alone it is confined, and where it is not found much if any below an altitude of 5,000 feet. Like the akakani, to which it is evidently related, the crested honey eater frequents the ohia trees almost exclusively and, like that bird, derives a large part of its subsistence from the nectar of the ohia flowers. Its long tube-like, brush-tipped tongue enables the bird to extract the honey from the tassel-like blossoms with great ease and celerity.

In midsummer, at least, *Palmeria* feeds to a considerable extent also upon insect food, especially upon the small green or brown caterpillars which at this season swarm upon both the ohia and koa trees. Upon these same caterpillars it also feeds its young which, by the middle of June, are fully fledged and mostly capable of caring for themselves, though still following their parents.

Palmeria is a strong and active bird, possessing a vigorous flight and displaying much activity in traversing the ohia branches, or in flitting from one cluster of blossoms to another. I noticed much animosity manifested by the individuals of this species towards the akakani. The habits of the two species are too much alike for friendly relations to exist, and the greater size and strength of *Palmeria* enable it to drive away its smaller rivals from coveted feeding grounds. Even the half-grown birds successfully attack the akakani, and divide their time between sipping honey and in chasing their rival cousins.

Like most of the honey-eating birds, the stomach of the crested honey eater is remarkably small for the size of the bird, so etherial a food as the nectar of flowers being speedily and easily digested and necessitating neither a capacious nor a strong stomach.

I heard no song at all from this species, though it is probable that in the mating season the bird gives musical utterance to its feelings. It is to be noted, however, that at the same time and in the same place both the akakani and iiwi were musical enough, though both species were feeding their young. *Palmeria* has a call note which is as characteristic as any sound heard in the Hawaiian woods. It is a loud, clear and rather shrill whistle, somewhat like a flycatcher's call (great crested flycatcher), but perhaps best described by comparison with the well known call of Bob White. The note is easily imitated, and the birds can invariably be induced to answer, and usually can be called up close to the observer. But for this fact *Palmeria* would be indeed difficult to discover, since it is neither numerous nor generally distributed but, on the contrary, is very local, the birds seeming to dwell in small, isolated communities.

The flight of the crested honey eater is unaccompanied by the rythmic pulsations so characteristic of the flight of the akakani (and of the iiwi) while its larger size and whitish crest, as well as the absence of the white crissum, serve to readily distinguish the bird from the former species.

I have mentioned the Drepanine characteristics of the tongue of *Palmeria,* but there is another Drepanine feature wanting in

all the specimens of *Palmeria* thus far examined by me. I allude
to the powerful scent noticeable in the case of every other member
of the group, and which I have come to consider as perfectly distinctive. I am assured, however, by Mr. Perkins that in his own
experience the *Drepanine* odor to the bird is very noticeable at
certain seasons. As the natives seem not to know the *Palmeria*
and to have no name for it, I suggest the above appellation.

Description.—Adult. Upper parts, wing and tail black; feathers of middle back and rump tipped with scarlet and with grayish shaft-streaks;
elbow and edge of wing scarlet, secondaries and greater wing coverts
tipped with grey; primaries edged with same; a broad nuchal band of
scarlet, extending over the side of neck; an occipital crest of pointed
lanceolate feathers black with light shaft streaks; a crest of dirty white
feathers, nearly an inch long, curved forward from the forehead and
partly covering the bill. A light scarlet ring around the eye, broadest
above. Throat and upper breast of a beautiful hoary grey; rest of under
parts black with grey shaft-streaks; feathers of belly and flanks tipped
with crimson; tibiae orange scarlet. Bills and legs black. Length about
7 inches. Female smaller.

The young repeat the pattern of coloration of the adult even to an incip-
ient crest, but the crimson is replaced by brownish pink. The legs are
brownish black, and the bill is black *with orange patches especially on the
lower mandible.*

Himatione sanguinea (Gmelin). Akakani; Apapani.

This is one of the most beautiful and abundant of the island
birds and, like the iiwi. is found upon all the islands.

In its general habits the akakani resembles the iiwi, but is
even more dependent for food upon the nectar of flowers than
that bird. Though perhaps a less persistent insect hunter the
year round than the iiwi, the akakani is dependent to a great
extent for a livelihood upon insects, and is extremely partial to the
little green and brown caterpillar of which nearly all the forest
birds are so fond.

Like the iiwi its feathers were much used in ancient times to
make cloaks, helmets and leis for the priests and lesser chiefs.

The akakani's song is sweet to the ear but is monotonous, and
is delivered at all seasons of the year and at all times of the day.
In fact this species and the iiwi rank as the most persistent song-

sters the writer has ever heard. The akakani has a delightful habit of gathering together in loose companies in the tops of the leafy ohia trees about midday, when hunger is appeased and most of the other forest songsters are silent, when the males join in a subdued lullaby and literally sing themselves and their mates to sleep.

The akakani usually nests in the tall forest ohias, but the writer has seen numerous nests in the small, scrubby ohias about the Volcano House which he attributed to this species; those examined were invariably empty.

Description.—Adult. Above and below crimson, brightest on the head and shading off on the abdomen into white; under tail coverts white; wing and tail black, the quills and secondaries edged with scarlet; under wing coverts ashy. Sexes practically indistinguishable. Length about 5¼ inches.

Himatione fraithii Rothschild. Laysan Akakani.

According to Palmer the akakani is by far the rarest of the Laysan birds, although it occurs in fair numbers. Like its relative it feeds upon the nectar of flowers though perhaps more dependent upon insects, of which it is an energetic hunter. According to Palmer the bird has a low sweet song.

The Laysan bird is no doubt a derivative of the Hawaiian Island stock, and must have been a resident of its present domain for a very long time.

Mr. Rothschild states that it resembles *sanguinea* of the islands, but has a shorter bill, and the color is scarlet vermilion instead of the darker blood-red of that species.

Ciridops anna (Dole). Ulaaihawane.

This beautiful and finch-like bird was first described by Mr. Dole from specimens taken on the island of Hawaii where alone the species has been found. These mounted birds, two in number, were in the collection of the late Mr. Mills and, presumably, were taken by the natives not far from Hilo, perhaps in the Olaa district. There is no evidence, however, of the exact locality whence they were derived, and it is possible that they may have come from some other part of the island.

No collector has met with the species recently, save a single individual shot for Mr. Palmer by a native on Mt. Kohala in February, 1892. From the fact that the principal food of the bird (as the natives say and as its name implies) was derived from the hawane palm, there would seem to be a reasonable hope that the bird may yet exist in the more elevated districts of the interior where alone this palm grows in abundance. However, even if the species is still extant is must be in very small numbers. To all intents and purposes the hawane finch may be looked upon as extinct, and as furnishing another melancholy example of the mysterious fate which has overtaken so many Hawaiian birds.

Description.—Adult. Crown black, shading into grey and white on the nape and sides of the neck; back brownish; lower breast, rump, upper tail-coverts, median and part of lesser coverts scarlet; throat and breast black, as also the tail, primaries and much of the secondaries.

Loxops coccinea (Gmelin). Akepeuie.

The members of this genus are the smallest of all Hawaiian birds and are among the most beautiful and most highly colored. This particular species is found only on the island of Hawaii where, in most districts, it is rather rare. In two regions only have I found the bird comparatively common, in the mixed ohia and koa forest on the north side of the Wailuku river at an altitude of some 1,800 feet upwards; and in the koa forest of Kau.

The bird is extremely partial to the koa tree, and its great rarity throughout the deep forests of Olaa is doubtless due to the general absence there of koa. The soft, small insects and caterpillars which constitute its chief food are almost entirely derived from the foliage of this acacia and from the foliage of the naio and mamane.

All the species of the genus *Loxops* possess symmetrical bills, the tip of the lower mandible having a decided twist to the right or left, as the case may be. No one, familiar with the curious crossed bills of the crossbills, and who has seen the birds manipulate pine seeds with these scissor-like instruments, could doubt for a moment that the peculiar bill of *Loxops* has originated in a similar way and has similar functions.

In his "Further Remarks on the Relations of the Drepanididae" in Wilsons' "The Birds of the Hawaiian Islands," Dr. Gadow refers to this peculiarity as follows: "Curiously enough, there exists another still more striking analogy between the crossbills and some Hawaiian birds, namely with *Loxops* incl. *Chrysomitridops.* As already known to Cabanis, when he established the genus Loxops, the under jaws of these little birds are not symmetrical—the distal half of the under jaw is twisted either to the right or to the left. It is interesting to note that the amount of twisting varies individually, right- and left-billed specimens occurring in equal numbers, and that it is smallest in young birds. There is not the slightest doubt that this asymmetry is acquired individually by their twisting open husks and seeds, or cracks of bark, in search of their food."

Notwithstanding the indicated function of the bill of *Loxops* and the apparent relation of cause and effect observable in its shape, the writer is bound to state that nothing in the habits of the bird, so far as he has been able to observe them, lends any color whatever to the theory; nor can he learn that Perkins' experience was different. As stated above *Loxops* hunts its prey among the leaves, the small, outermost twigs, and the flowers of the koa, but never, so far as the writer is aware, probes into the cracks and crevices of the bark for food nor twists off "husks and seed." The bird may, indeed, possess these latter habits, as its bill indicates it should, but none of the thirty or forty individuals the writer has seen have thus been employed, nor do the contents of the many stomachs he has examined contradict his observations.

Moreover, the peculiar twist of the bill does not seem to be in any wise dependent on age but, on the contrary, is as apparent in some ten or fifteen individuals in juvenile plumage as it is in the oldest individuals. Individually, however, the birds differ much in the extent to which the bill is twisted.

The writer can but regret that he has no theory of his own to propose in place of the one above given which, however sound and plausible it may appear, seems not to accord with observations in the field.

The curiosity of this little bird is remarkable and, by making odd, squeaking notes, the writer has more than once called a pair down from the top of a tall koa to within a few feet of him when he had no idea that there was an akepeuie within miles. It is probable that certain small nests common in the outermost twigs of the topmost branches of the koa belong to this species but he has no definite proof of the fact.

Like many other Hawaiian birds, the akepeuie pairs at an early age, while still in the juvenile dress. There appears to be much individual difference in plumage in all stages, particularly that of the adult, or, at least, of the breeding, females.

In the introduction to these pages brief reference is made (p. 20) to certain tumors or swellings affecting the feet and the soft parts round the bill of Hawaiian birds. A specimen was forwarded to Washington for investigation, and the following report has been received from D. E. Salmon, Chief of the Bureau of Animal Industry: "I am in receipt of your letter of September 11th together with a specimen of a bird, *Loxops coccinea,* affected with tumor-like growths on the head, feet and thighs. You state that this disease is very prevalent among the various woodland birds in the Hawaiian Islands, and request that you be furnished with information concerning the nature and cause of the disease.

In reply I would say that a microscopical examination has demonstrated the presence within the degenerated tissues of numerous fungoid growths which closely resemble morphologically the blastomyctes described by Sanfelice in his article, Uber die pathogene wirkung der Blastomyceten, published in Zeit. fur Hygiene und Infectionskrankheiten, 1897, page 298.

These organisms have been demonstrated during the past summer in diseased chickens which were forwarded from Honolulu, and this fact adds to the probability of the same microphyte being the causative agent in the disease under consideration. This affection, commonly called chicken pox, sore head and bird pox, has been known for many years and is usually found in warm countries, especially in Southern Europe and the Gulf Section of the United States. It affects ordinary fowls, turkeys, pigeons and birds, and Bollinger, Virchow's Archiv. Bd. LVIII, S. 349, mentions an outbreak among hawks and pheasants.

Further information concerning the disease may be found in Bulletin No. 1, of the Hawaii Agricultural Experiment Station, entitled "Chickens and their Diseases in Hawaii."

With reference to the foregoing it may be remarked that if the disease in question be the same that prevails so extensively among the domestic fowls of the islands, it seems to assume a much milder type among the wild birds, whether native or introduced. If it resulted in blindness and death among wild birds as frequently for instance as it does among chickens, the fact would hardly have escaped the attention of observers.

The writer has examined scores of wild birds that were affected with these tumors when they were shot, or had been affected previously, but none of them showed serious impairment of health and vigor. The disease must often prove a serious inconvenience to wild birds, but apparently it is rarely or never the cause of death.

Description.—Adult male. Color above scarlet orange, duller on the back. Beneath cadmium-orange, brighter on the belly, wing and tail dusky brown, each feather and the wing coverts edged with orange. Bill pale yellow, sometimes orange-yellow at base; tip dusky; legs and feet blackish brown. Length about 4.5 inches.

Adult female. Above dull olive-green, brighter on forehead, rump and upper tail-coverts; wing and tail quills blackish brown margined with greenish olive as also the secondaries. Below beautiful gamboge-yellow, paler on abdomen. This is the extreme adult phase of the adult female and is very rare. More usually the gamboge underneath is limited to breast and throat, the upper parts being much duller than described. In juvenile specimens the head is dull olive grey. Back washed with olive-green; under parts ashy grey, tinged with pale yellowish.

Loxops rufa (Bloxham.). Oahu Akepeuie.

Found only on Oahu where it is now very rare and probably soon will be extinct. It is distinguished from allied species of other islands by its more brownish color and its smaller size.

Loxops ochracea Rothschild.   Ochraceus Akepeuie.

My own experience with the Maui akepeuie is rather limited.
I found it in June to be rather rare on the slopes of Haleakala,
frequenting scattered koa trees which are here not at all common.
No doubt the bird is more numerous in localities where the koa
abounds.   The akepeuie formed little family groups, the fully
fledged young accompanying their parents, now in the moult, in
their search for food.   The food of this, as of the other species,
consists chiefly of caterpillars and very small spiders.   These they
obtain almost wholly from among the leaves of the koa, though
occasionally the akepeuie is found hunting in the ohia trees.   Mr.
Perkins saw this species and L. cæruleirostris sucking the nectar
of the ohia flowers, but rarely.

Mr. Perkins remarks that the different species of *Loxops* "have
much the same habits, and the song, which is short and simple,
though sweet, is nearly the same in all.   Their call is a plain
keewit, uttered once or repeated, and is constantly heard."

Description.—Adult male.   Dark orange above, becoming lighter
(orange-ochraceus) on the rump and belly and under tail-coverts; wings
and tail dusky brown edged with orange-yellow.   Bill slate-blue, tip blackish.   Legs plumbeus.   Length about 4½ inches.

Adult female.   Above dark green, lighter on the rump; wings and tail
dusky black edged with yellowish green; below light yellow washed with
dusky green on the sides and throat.

Loxops cæruleirostris (Wilson).   Ou-holowai.

This fine species was discovered by Mr. Wilson upon the island
of Kauai at an elevation of about 3,000 feet.   So far as known
the bird is confined to this island.   According to its describer, the
ou-holowai has a siskin-like song which distinguishes it from
Chlorodrepanis parva, in whose company it was usually found,
frequenting the low branches of the ohias.

Description.—Adult.   Crown and under parts gamboge yellow; occiput,
back, upper surface of wings, and tail greenish olive, brighter on rump.
Lores black, extending to base of bill above and below.   Wing and tail
quills dusky brown.   Bill light prussian blue; feet bluish black.   Length
about 4.5 inches.

Pseudonestor xanthophrys Rothschild. Parrot-billed Koa Finch.

This extraordinary and finch-like bird is found only on the island of Maui where it is very local and is confined to the high forest from an elevation of about 4,000 feet upward.

The formidable, hooked and parrot-like bill suggests peculiar and remarkable habits, a suggestion fully confirmed by observation of the bird in the midst of its natural surroundings. Mr. Perkins has given an admirable account of Pseudonestor's habits, and my own experience with the bird in the forests of Haleakala fully confirm the accuracy of his observations.

The bird appears never to wander far from the koa, and obtains the principal part of its food, the larvae of longicorn beetles, by tearing open the small terminal dead twigs of this tree in which the larvae burrow, secure from all bird enemies less formidably equipped. The stout legs and claws of the bird enable it to maintain its hold on the branches in any desired position and for any length of time, and a suspected twig is soon reduced to fragments by the operation of its powerful mandibles.

Undoubtedly, as suggested by Mr. Perkins, the peculiar bill of *Pseudonestor* and its powerful jaw muscles have been developed by use in the above manner.

I found the bird in June feeding its young, and at this time it has recourse, as have so many other Hawaiian species, to the little caterpillars which infest the koa and ohia at all seasons of the year but, especially, in the summer. In its search for these the bird descends into the shrubbery to within a few feet of the ground.

Pseudonestor is very tame and unsuspicious and withal a bit curious, and while at work may be watched at short range more easily than any Hawaiian bird known to me.

Like so many other Hawaiian birds this species is very local, but unlike some others it is rare, and I never saw more than two in a long day's search, more frequently none at all. All the individuals that came under my notice, less than ten in all, were silent save one male which as it flew emitted a low faint pea, much like the call of *Chlorodrepanis virens,* which was probably the call to

its young. Mr. Perkins, however, heard from it "a decided song"
which he likens to that of the amakihi.

The koa upon Maui has suffered much of late years from the
ravages of the insect pests above alluded to, and thousands of
mature trees have been killed. The life of *Pseudonestor* is so in-
separably connected with the koa tree that the destruction of the
latter will be almost certainly followed by the extinction of the
former, and it is to be feared that this interesting and valuable
bird, confined as it is to one island, has before it no very long
term of existence.

The powerful odor which attaches to the plumage of so many
of the *Drepanididæ* is very marked in the case of this bird, being
nearly, or quite, as strong as in the ou.

Description.—Adult. Upper parts green, suffused with grey; head and
rump brighter; wings and tail brown edged with green; a broad superciliary streak of canary yellow from bill to nape. Under parts canary
yellow; sides and flanks green. Maxilla bluish black, cutting edge
whitish; mandible whitish; legs plumbeus, soles yellowish.

Female smaller and duller. Length of adult about 5½ inches.

The young bird in juvenile dress is colored much like the adult, but is
pale yellowish underneath.

Psittırostra psittacea (Gmelin). Ou.

The ou is one of the winged gems of the island forests, and
happily is widely distributed throughout the group. It is found
on all the larger islands, including even Lanai, although upon
Oahu it is now practically extinct.

The bright green plumage of the ou, its yellow head and its
powerful beak combine to suggest to the uninitiated the parrot
family; in fact the bird was called by Latham, its first describer,
the "Parrot-billed Grosbeak."

The ou is, perhaps, the only really fine songster among the
island birds, and in the writer's opinion its song far excels that of
any other Hawaiian species. The song is somewhat suggestive of
that of the canary's and in Olaa it is the general belief that the
woods are full of escaped cage birds. Yet in power, sweetness and
melodiousness the song of the ou at its best far excels the canary's.
Unfortunately the ou is rather chary of its melody, and its finished

performances are less frequently heard than snatches and bits of song, dropped carelessly, as it were, by the way-side while the bird is pursuing its regular avocations.

The powerful, hooked bill suggests a special use, and this use is made apparent when the bird is at work prying out from the spadix the seeds of the ieie, which constitute the special food of the ou. The ease and celerity with which this task is accomplished sufficiently attest the purpose of the instrument and its efficiency. The bird is very fond also of mamaki berries, which seem to make up a large part of the subsistence of the young, at least after they get fairly on the wing. The ou eats, also, many other kinds of berries, such as the alani, kopiko, kawau and others. It feeds, also, upon bananas and guavas, and the late Mr. E. Hitchcock informed me that the first year his peach trees bore the ou paid them marked attention, apparently fully approving of this, to it, new kind of fruit.

In connection with the love of the bird for small fruits, it is to be remarked that it seems to pay no attention whatever to the raspberries, originally imported from Jamaica, which have overrun the whole of Olaa, and are everywhere very abundant. The ou seems not to be at all partial to insect food at any time of year, though occasionally I have found larvae of several kinds in its stomach.

The ou is a common and generally distributed species in the ohia forests of the island of Hawaii from about 1,000 feet upwards, and presumably its range in the other islands is the same. It is generally found in small companies, never singly. Like most, perhaps all Hawaiian birds, the ou seems to be always paired, and I believe it is the rule that all Hawaiian birds pair for life. The ou has a pretty and plaintive call-note, much like that of the American goldfinch and, as it is easily and accurately imitated, the presence of the birds may always be detected by means of it. Perched in the tops of ohias or hidden by the clustering leaves of the ieie, the birds will continue to answer the call almost indefinitely, all the while peering about with an air of innocent wonder and surprise. Though the bird is so common nothing has yet been learned of its nest and eggs.

5-H B

Description.—Adult male. Head and neck gamboge-yellow; back, edges of secondaries of remiges, and rectrices olive-green, brighter on rump and upper tail-coverts; wing-coverts, remiges and rectrices blackish brown. Under parts olive-grey washed with olive-green, especially on the sides and flanks; belly greyish white; under tail-coverts grey washed with green; bill white with faint bluish tinge; legs flesh color. Length about 6.30 inches.

Adult female. Above olive-green, brighter on head and rump; feathers of back with dark olive centers. Beneath smoky grey, passing into white on abdomen; sides and flanks olive-green.

Juvenile plumage. Above dark olive-green; beneath a lighter shade of same, washed with yellow on throat; lower breast and belly sulphur-yellow.

Psittirostra olivacea Rothschild. Oahu Ou.

At one time, no doubt, the ou was as common upon the island of Oahu as it now is on most of the other islands. In 1893 Mr. Perkins saw a pair there, and Mr. Bryan informs us (Key of the Birds of the Hawaiian Group, p. 54) that he saw an individual in Moanalua valley as late as October, 1899. A few pairs may still linger here and there. Still the bird is to be looked upon as practically extinct on Oahu.

The cause of the extinction of the ou upon Oahu seems to be very obscure. The fruit of the ieie vine is the particular food of the bird, and there are considerable tracts of timber on the mountains of the island where this vine still abounds. So, too, there are sections where the guava and the mamaki are still plentiful, and the ou is very fond of their fruit and berries. There apparently being no scarcity of food and shelter, why should the ou have disappeared from Oahu, and yet persist upon other islands where the timbered areas are even more restricted?

The Oahu bird appears not to differ in any important particular from *psittacea*, and perhaps, as suggested by Mr. Rothschild, is to be distinguished sub-specifically rather than specifically. The chief differences, as indicated by Mr. Rothschild, are the buffy whitish breast, abdomen and under tail-coverts of adult males of olivacea, the breast being washed with olive and the sides olive-green as contrasted with the olive-green under parts of adult psittacea, the whitish being restricted to the middle of the lower abdomen. The wing of the Oahu form is also said to be shorter and the upper side to have a more olive tint.

Loxioides bailleui Oustalet   Palila.

While in general appearance so much resembling the ou that the natives frequently confound the two and call both ou, the present species differs in many important particulars, especially in the size and shape of the bill.

The palila is not only limited to the island of Hawaii but, so far as is known, is confined to the districts of Kona and Hamakua where it lives in the upper woods. Here it is said to subsist upon the seeds of the mamane tree. This tree is not common on the windward side of the island, not being found at all in the lower woods, and this fact may explain the bird's absence there.

Mr. Wilson heard no song from the palila. It had, however, a clear whistle-like note which, when often repeated, is held by the natives to be a sign of approaching rain. Should the palila prove on further investigation to be without song, the fact will be a remarkable one in the light of the decided musical powers of its relative, the ou.

Description.—Adult male. Head and neck deep gamboge-yellow; rest of upper surface ashy grey, lighter on the rump; wing-coverts, rectrices and tetrices dusky black, edged with olive-yellow. Throat and upper part of breast gamboge-yellow; rest of under surface dusk white; bill and feet slaty purple. Length about 6.5 inches. Female duller.

Telespiza cantans Wilson.   Laysan Finch.

According to Rothschild the Laysan finch is common all over the island of Laysan, to which it is confined. "They are quite omnivorous, eating insects and other birds' eggs, and seem fond of bathing in water. Mr. Freeth says he has seen a small flock feeding on a dead albatross." The nests were built of grass and small twigs and were placed in the scrub or in the tussocks of grass. They nest about May, and lay from two to four eggs. Many of these birds are brought to Honolulu in cages, and sold for cage birds. They thrive well for a time but ultimately die, perhaps from the lack of their accustomed varied diet. The song is sweet but not very spirited.

The *T. flavissima* of Rothschild is now admitted by that author to be only the extreme adult phase of the present species.

Description.—Adult. Head, neck and under parts to lower abdomen rich yellow; upper parts brown, more or less washed with yellowish, and with or without dark streakings on middle back; wing-coverts brown. they with primaries and secondaries margined with yellow; abdomen whitish; tail feathers dark brown, margined with yellow; bill horn color; legs and feet blackish brown. Juvenile birds are browner, and are streaked above and below. Length about 6.50 inches.

Rhodacanthis palmeri Rothschild. Hopue; Orange Koa Finch.

This, the largest and finest of all the Hawaiian finch-like forms, is confined to the island of Hawaii, where it seems to be restricted to the western side, or to the districts of Kona and Kau. It is known chiefly from Kona, but Mr. Perkins informs me that he saw numbers of the bird in the extensive koa woods above the volcano. This locality is on the very edge of the rainy Olaa district which the bird appears never to enter.

The koa finch seems not to descend to low altitudes but to be found from about 4,000 feet upwards. It frequents chiefly the forests of koa, the beans of which constitute its principal food. Mr. Perkins, to whom we now owe most of our knowledge of the habits of the species, says "It does not restrict itself to the koa bean, but varies its diet by feeding on lepidopterous larvae, just as the Psittacirostra does." "Its peculiar whistle, though not very loud, is very clear, and can be heard for a considerable distance. If imitated closely it will readily answer and sometimes, after fruitless search for hours without even hearing a sound from this bird, a whistle has been immediately responded to."

Description.—Adult male. Head, throat and under parts reddish orange, duller on the abdomen; back and upper wing-coverts dull greenish olivaceus. Wing and tail blackish brown. Length about 8¾ inches.

The female is duller; above olive-green, brighter on the forehead. Throat and sides of body olive-green; breast and abdomen dull white washed with green.

Rhodacanthis flaviveps, Rothschild. Yellow-headed Koa Finch.

This species was described by Mr. Rothschild from two specimens obtained by Mr. Palmer in Kona in the same locality inhabited by the previous bird. The present form is supposed to be
smaller and with much yellow and green in its plumage. Notwithstanding these differences, until more specimens have been procured, the exact status of the bird can hardly be regarded as
settled.

Description.—Adult male. Head, neck and underparts apple-yellow,
brighter and richer on the head and neck, and greener on the under
parts. Upper parts ashy green, becoming bright green on the lower
back, rump and upper tail-coverts; wings and tail dull blackish brown,
the feathers margined with green. Female duller and greener. Length
about 7.5 inches. (Rothschild.)

Chloridops kona, Wilson. Palila.

This remarkable finch is one of the most local of all Hawaiian
birds, and is confined to the Kona district of the island of Hawaii.
Mr. Perkins seems to have enjoyed better opportunities for observing its habits than anyone else, and the following is taken
from his account of the species in the "Ibis." The palila "though an
interesting bird on account of its peculiar structure is a singularly
uninteresting one in its habits. It is a dull, sluggish, solitary,
bird, and very silent—its whole existence may be summed up in
the words 'to eat.' Its food consists of the seeds of the fruit of
the aaka (bastard sandal-tree, and probably at other seasons of
those of the sandal-wood tree), and as these are very minute, its
whole time seems to be taken up in cracking the extremely hard
shells of this fruit, for which its extraordinarily powerful beak
and heavy head have been developed. * * * The incessant
cracking of the fruits when one of these birds is feeding, the noise
of which can be heard for a considerable distance, renders the
bird much easier to get than it otherwise would be. It is mostly
found on the roughest lava, but also wanders into the open spaces
of the forest."

Description.—Adult male. Above and below bright olive-green; lores dusky; abdomen whitish. Length about 6 inches. Female similar.

MELIPHAGIDÆ. HONEY-SUCKER FAMILY.

Moho nobilis (Merrem.). O-O.

This magnificent species, a prince among Hawaiian birds, inhabits the island of Hawaii where, in former times, it was widespread throughout the lower as well as the middle forest. Today it is fast nearing extermination.

This species, and the much rarer mamo, yielded the yellow feathers so precious in the eyes of the higher Hawaiian chiefs, and it is to obtain possession of the coveted feathers that the birds have been sacrificed. True, it is said to have been the practice of the ancient bird-catchers to release their captives after plucking the golden harvest under each wing and tail, each bird yielding fifty feathers and upwards. Moreover dire penalties are said to have followed the detection of an infraction of this law.

It is not to be overlooked, however, that the brilliant shining black body feathers of the o-o were also in great demand for making cloaks and, as remarked by Prof. Brigham, the bird could hardly survive the loss of nearly its entire plumage. It may well be, therefore, that the old bird catchers were not wholly unacquainted with the good qualities of the flesh of the o-o, which is said to be most excellent eating.

The above merciful and wise custom, if ever generally observed, (there is no doubt that a law prohibiting the killing of the o-o was made by Kamehameha) died out together with the chiefs with whom it originated and with the old race of bird-catchers. The silent snare has given place to the deadly shot gun. Though island royalty is no more, the demand for feather leis continues, and to meet it the o-o has been pursued till only a few remain in the distant woodland fastnesses—so few and so shy from persecution that happily the yield to the lei hunter no longer repays the labor and trouble of pursuit.

The districts of Olaa and Puna are today almost absolutely tenantless of this beautiful bird, where formerly there were multitudes. As late as 1898 more than one thousand individuals of this species were shot by the lei hunters in the heavily wooded district north of the Wailuku river, where their presence had probably been overlooked. Having been undisturbed for some years the birds were increasing rapidly, and doubtless in time might have reoccupied their lost territory in other districts. But the rapacity of the lei-hunters leaves little hope for the future of this beautiful and interesting bird, and the district alluded to is now almost depopulated.

The extermination of the o-o is the more to be regretted inasmuch as the bird is a very active and persistent insect destroyer, on which account it can the less be spared from the Hawaiian woods. In the stomachs of most of those I have dissected I have found the remains of beetles, flies and coleopterous larvæ. In addition to insects, which I feel sure are its principal food, the o-o is fond of bananas. It also feeds much at times upon the nectar of flowers. Wilson says that in captivity it has been kept on the juice of the sugar cane, but I do not believe that the bird's existence could be long prolonged on such thin fare*

In connection with its food, I may add that the stomach of the o-o is astonishingly small for the size of the bird, and is but little, if any, larger than that of the iivi which is a much smaller bird.

The o-o usually frequents the tops of the tallest trees where it glides over the branches with marvellous celerity, now and then stopping to utter its far reaching call and to jet its long tail. This latter action serves to reveal its bright yellow under tail-coverts to its no doubt admiring mate, and it is probable, though I have not been able to verify the supposition, that its wings are frequently opened to display the similar adornment under them. The latter, of course, are always visible when the bird is flying.

Upon one or two occasions only, by the use of great caution, I

---

*Since the above was written the writer has had further opportunities for observing the o-o, and is inclined to believe that when obtainable the nectar of flowers, especially of the ohia, forms a very important part of the food of the bird, though it always supplements its liquid fare by the more substantial one of insects. The latter probably are absolutely essential to the bird's existence.

have succeeded in getting close to a small company of these birds, and have watched them unsuspected. This was soon after daylight, and they were feeding among the lower branches of the ohias, and even in the shrubbery, a practice no doubt common with them formerly. The moment the birds learned of my presence they showed the greatest agitation, and at once retreated to the tops of the tallest forest trees, which persecution has taught them is their only safe refuge.

When feeding in the early morning, and particularly when with their young, the calls of the o-o are almost incessant, and it is this loud and constantly repeated call-note which has led to the easy destruction of the species.

The poor bird has yet to learn that its appreciation of the joyousness of existence and its love for its mate and young can be expressed only at the cost of its very life. Thrice happy o-o in the olden days when its tribute to royalty was unstained with its life blood.

After nine in the morning the o-o usually lapses into absolute silence, save for an occasional note from dream-land as the bird slumbers in the tops of the tallest trees where it is entirely invisible. The note—the bird apparently has no song—is a loud double syllabled chook, chook, but neither these syllables, nor any others, can convey an adequate idea of the sound of the bird's voice or represent its peculiar rhythm, which is not without ventriloquial quality, and always sounds much nearer than it actually is. None of the present day natives whom I have asked have been able to imitate the call of the o-o though it is said, and no doubt truly, that in ancient times this accomplishment was a prerequisite to the honorable and lucrative practice of bird catching. However, the writer has succeeded in whistling a rude semblance of the note, and many times has elicited a response, even where before he was not aware of the bird's presence. It must be added, however, that the bird has always detected the cheat after a repetition or two, and has declined further responses.

The o-o breeds in the late spring and early summer, retiring for this purpose into the depths of the middle forest, and no doubt places its nest in the tops of the tallest ohias. After the young are on the wing, both old and young associate in large companies, and there is a definite and decided movement from higher to lower ground. I have found large companies thus gathered to-gether late in August and early in September on the outermost edge of the woods, the young apparently being still in attendance on their parents. At such times the calls and answering calls are incessant.

Description.—Adult. Head and occiput purplish, shining black, the feathers stiff and imbricated so as to give the effect of speckling; upper parts generally shining black, the bases of the body feathers duller black, producing a variegated effect; the neck feathers have a brownish cast, giving the effect in some lights of a broad nuchal collar; behind the malars and encroaching on the ear-spaces is a band of iridescent brown. Beneath shining black, the feathers having the same variegated appearance as above; belly with a tinge of brown; under wing-coverts (of about 20 feathers each) and under tail coverts bright yellow; anal tuft white; two outer tail feathers on each side white for about half their length; bases, black, as also the shafts at tip; middle pair of rectrices twisted outwardly on their axes near the tip. Length about 12.5 inches.

Female. Similar in color to the male, though not so bright, and with the middle pair of rectrices much shorter and but little twisted. Length about 9.5.

Juvenile plumage. Dull black all over.

Moho apicalis (Gould). Oahu O-O.

This, the o-o of Oahu no doubt was formerly common, but none of the recent explorers have found it, and the presumption is that it is now extinct, a presumption rendered all the more probable from the extensive deforestation which has occurred on that island; for the o-o is preeminently a bird of the dense forest.

Description.—Adult male. Black. Back and rump brownish and with distinct shaft lines. Rectrices with white tips for from one-half to an inch. Breast, flanks, vent and under tail-coverts yellow. Under wing-coverts white.

Moho bishopi, Rothschild. Molokai O-O.

This o-o has been found only upon the island of Molokai. As yet nothing has been published upon its habits which presumably do not differ essentially from those of its congeners.

The species may yet, however, be found to occur on the
island of Maui from which, hitherto, no species of moho has
been reported. On June 9, 1901, however, I saw a single adult
male o-o in the forest tract northeast of Olinda, at an elevation of
about 4,500 feet. I was close to the bird, saw it plainly, and heard
its notes distinctly, and am positive as to its identification as one
of the members of this genus. The species has yet to be determined but, if not an undescribed species, it is likely to prove to
be *bishopi,* and to be common to both Maui and Molokai, as is
the *Palmeria dolei.*

Description.—Adult male. Upper parts black with a brownish tinge on
back; underparts brownish black, the feathers of the latter and of the
hind neck being lanceolate and having whitish shaft-streaks. A tuft of
feathers with long golden yellow tips springs from near the ear-coverts
and is directed backwards; axillary tufts and under til-coverts gamboge-
yellow. Length about 8.62 inches. Female smaller.

Moho braccatus (Cassin). O-O A-A.

This bird, known as the dwarf o-o is confined to the island of
Kauai where, according to Wilson, it is found at all elevations of
the forest and is by no means uncommon. The coveted yellow
feathers are confined, in this species, to a small patch upon either
thigh, and hence the bird was little persecuted as compared with
its relative on Hawaii.

The late Mr. Knudsen reported that the species, as was to be
expected, is fond of bananas. Mr. Wilson observed it feeding
upon the nectar of ohia flowers and of those of the tree lobelia.
I have no doubt that the dwarf o-o feeds much also upon insects.

According to Wilson this species "has a sweet song, some of
its notes possessing a bell-like clearness."

In his notes upon this species Mr. Rothschild remarks that
"these birds have a remarkable and somewhat musk-like scent,
even strongly perceptible in a box of skins. The same scent is
present in the other species of *Moho.*"

I feel positive that in ascribing a strong odor to any of the
species of this genus Mr. Rothschild is mistaken. Without doubt
the odor noticed by him from the *Moho* skins, which he likens to

the well known musky scent of the *Drepanine* birds, originated with the latter and was communicated from them in the shipping box or in the cabinet. The odor from freshly made skins of the *Drepanididæ* is exceedingly penetrating, as well as lasting, and will attach to any object confined with them. Freshly killed specimens of *Moho* have no perceptible odor. I have had in hand over a dozen freshly killed *M. nobilis,* and they are absolutely unscented. Moreover Mr. Perkins, who has shot *braccatus,* as well as *nobilis* and *bishopi,* informs me that none of these species possess the Drepanine odor.

The matter has considerable interest since, up to the present time, no Hawaiian bird has been found to possess this peculiar musky scent, save only the members of the *Drepanididæ,* and they all have it in perceptible degree.

It might at first seem that this peculiar odor, so unlike that of other birds, is peculiar to the islands, and is derived from the food of the birds. The several members of the Drepanine Family, however, differ so much in regard to their food, as to render such a supposition hardly tenable. Moreover, there are other birds, in nowise related to the Drepanine Family, as the several species of *Moho,* of *Chasiempis,* and of *Phæornis,* which live upon much the same fare as the Drepanids, and yet are without the peculiar scent of the latter.

There seems, therefore, good reason to conclude that this odor, universal among the Drepanids and absent in all the other island birds, indicates a common ancestry for the former, and may yet prove a sufficient clew to their original home whence they migrated to the islands.

Description.—Adult male. Head black, feathers stiff and lanceolate; above slaty brown, lighter on rump; interscapularies with light shaft-streaks; wing and tail black, central pair of rectrices much exceeding the rest; anterior edge of wing white; chin, throat and upper breast black, with tranverse sub-apical bars of white; rest of under parts slaty brown; feathers of lower breast with light shaft-streaks; lower thigh chrome-yellow. Length about 7.75 inches.

Female similar but with whiter throat.

Chaetoptila angustipluma (Peale).

This remarkable species was secured by Peale of the U. S. exploring expedition, and was described in 1848. The following is his brief account of it: "This rare species was obtained at the Island of Hawaii. It is very active and graceful in its motions, frequents the woody districts, and is disposed to be musical, having most of the habits of a *Meliphaga*. They are generally found about those trees which are in flower."

Mr. Mills, formerly of Hilo, also procured at least two specimens of the bird, presumably from natives living in Olaa. I have many times visited the Olaa woods and have spent many days there, always having the bird in mind, but have seen no trace of it.

Of the several species known formerly to have inhabited the island of Hawaii and now supposed to be extinct, the case of the *Chaetoptila* is perhaps the most hopeless as regards the chance of survivors. A bird of such large size, of active habits and musical can hardly have escaped attention all these years. It has been seen by no one since the time of Mr. Mills, and the natives do not know it even by name.

It was doubtless confined to a limited district in Hawaii, for no one has been able to verify the statement of Mr. Dole (Hawaiian Annual for 1879, p. 47) that the bird was found in Molokai as well.

Description.—Top of the head and neck blackish brown, each feather with a greyish white shaft-streak which is strongly tinged with yellow on the nape and sides of the neck. A greyish-white stripe over the eyes. Wing-coverts and back hair brown, tinged with ochreous on the rump, the feathers of the mantle with a white shaft-streak widening into a tear-shaped spot towards the tip; remiges and rectrices deep brown, their outer margin yellow, giving a greenish effect to the whole. A greyish-white stripe over the eye. Lores, sides of the head and ear-coverts dull black, the feathers immediately under the eye mottled with greyish white. Chin and throat dull white, tinged with yellow, the shafts and the hairs with which this part is beset black. Breast and abdomen dull white, striped longitudinally with darkish brown; flanks strongly tinged with ochreous. Length about 13 inches. (Wilson.)

ACEDINIDÆ. KINGFISHER FAMILY.

Ceryle alcyon (Linn.). Belted Kingfisher.

Early in November of 1901 the attention of Mr. Harry Patten, of Hakalau, was called by some natives to the presence of a pair of strange birds in the mouth of Hakalau Gulch. Mr. Patten visited the locality, and at once identified the birds as belted kingfishers. They seemed to be quite at home amid their novel surroundings, perching on a telephone wire much of the time, and evidently reaping a satisfactory harvest of small fish from the stream.

One of them, however, disappeared, having probably been shot, and on the 27th of the month Mr. W. K. Andrews, of Honomu, went to the gulch, and secured the remaining bird, kindly presenting it to the writer.

It proved to be an adult female, and as the other bird is said to have been somewhat differently colored it was, no doubt, a male.

So far as the writer is aware this is the first reported occurrence of the species in the islands. It is in the late fall months that most of the strays from the American coast reach the group, and this pair was undoubtedly blown off the coast during the fall migration, and lured hither in the company of plover or other regular migrants to the islands.

The occurrences of stray mainland birds in the group is of great interest, and should always be reported by sportsmen, to whom the knowledge usually comes, since they indicate the manner and the sources whence the original avian inhabitants of the islands were derived. It is rarely that strays reach the islands in pairs, as these kingfishers appear to have done, and, had the birds chanced to reach a more isolated section, it is possible they might have chosen to remain and so have founded a colony of their kind.

Description.—Adult male. Above bluish plumbeous; tail with tranverse white markings; primaries with spots of same; forehead with white spot; below white, with band of plumbeous across breast; white of throat encircling hind-neck. Female similar, but sides and flanks rufous, with an interrupted band of same across belly. Length 11.00-14.50.

BUBONIDÆ. OWL FAMILY.

Asio accipitrinus sandwichensis (Bloxam). Pueo. Short-eared
    Owl.

That the pueo must have been long a resident of the islands is
evident both because the bird is diffused throughout the entire
group and because it figures prominently in Hawaiian folk-lore,.
the bird being formerly worshipped as a God, one of the poe akua.
mana.

The following is a fair specimen of the animal myths current in
ancient Hawaii, and illustrates the place held by the owl in Hawaiian mythology :*

"There lived a man named Kapoi, at Kahehuna, in Honolulu,
who one day went to Kewalo to get some thatching for his house.
On his way back he found some owl's eggs which he gathered together and brought home with him; in the evening he wrapped
them in *ti leaves* and was about to roast them in hot ashes when
an owl perched on the fence which surrounded his house and called
out to him, "O Kapoi! give me my eggs." Kapoi asked the owl,
"How many eggs had you?" "Seven eggs," replied the owl.
Kapoi then said, "Well! I wish to roast these eggs for my sup-
per." The owl asked the second time for its eggs and was
answered by Kapoi in the same manner. Then said the owl, "O
heartless Kapoi! why don't you take pity on me? Give me my
eggs." Kapoi then told the owl to come and take them.

The owl having got the eggs told Kapoi to build up a *heiau*
(temple), and instructed him to make an altar and call the temple
by the name of Manua. Kapoi built the temple, as directed; set
kapu days for its dedication and placed the customary sacrifice on
the altar.

News spread to the hearing of Kakuihewa, who was then King
of Oahu, living at the time at Waikiki, that a certain man had
kapued certain days for his *heiau,* and had already dedicated it.
This King had made a law that whoever among his people should

---

*From the *Hawaiian Annual* for 1892.

ASIO ACCIPITRINUS SANDWICHENSIS. SHORT EARED OWL, PUEO.

erect a *heiau* and kapu the same before the King had his temple kapued, that man should pay the penalty of death. Kapoi was thereupon seized, by the King's orders, and led to the *heiau* of Kupalaha, at Waikiki.

That same day, the owl that had told Kapoi to erect a temple gathered all the owls from Lanai, Maui, Molokai and Hawaii to one place at Kalapueo.[1] All those from the Koolau districts were assembled at Kanoniakapueo,[2] and those from Kauai and Niihau at Pueohulunui.[3]

It was decided by the King that Kapoi should be put to death on the day of Kane.[4] When that day came, at daybreak, the owls left their places of rendezvous and covered the whole sky over Honolulu, and as the King's servants seized Kapoi to put him to death the owls flew at them, pecking with their beaks and scratching them with their claws. Then and there the battle was fought between Kakuihewa's people and the owls. At last the owls conquered and Kapoi was released, the King acknowledging that his *Akua* (God) was a powerful one. From that time the owl has been recognized as one of the many deities venerated by the Hawaiian people."

The recent examination of a large amount of material in the way of skins from the islands and from abroad has led Rothschild to consider the island bird as a distinct form, distinguishable chiefly by its smaller size. Six specimens of my own collecting confirm his measurements.

According to Andrew's Dictionary there was a special form of snare designed for catching the owl, called pehe or peheapueo, "snare for catching owls." It is possible that owl's feathers were employed for decorative purposes, but it is more probable that the feathers taken from the captured owls were used to decorate the owl idols, or employed as offerings to propitiate the owl god's favor. Nor is it improbable that owls were kept captive in the heiaus or temples.

The pueo was formerly very numerous in the lowlands of all the islands, but the extension of the canefields has materially

---

[1] Situate beyond Diamond Head. [2] In Nuuanu Valley. [3] Near Moanalua. [4] When the moon is 27 days old.

diminished its numbers by depriving the bird of suitable nesting sites. Moreover the owl has ruthlessly been killed of late years, for no other reason than that it is an owl. As a result the pueo is nowadays getting comparatively rare. This is unfortunate, especially for the cane and coffee growers, since rats and mice are this owl's chief, nay almost its only food, and it annually destroys vast numbers of these mischievous rodents

That it eats lizards, occasionally at least, is proved by the fact that one which I dissected in Kau had in its crop, in addition to a good sized rat, two lizards (*Peropus mutilatus* and *Lepidodactylus garnotti*).

No one alleges mischievous habits against the pueo. It kills no poultry, or does so only exceptionally, and harms no one, and the bird should be protected by law and preserved for the good it is continually doing.

Its native name, pueo, is a good rendering of its cry which it commonly utters as it hunts in the early morning hours or the late afternoon. The bird sees uncommonly well in the daytime, and not rarely is abroad in bright sunlight; nor does it fly after dark, unless by moonlight.

Its habit of remaining stationary some little distance above the ground on rapidly moving wings, as it anxiously scans the ground beneath for mice, is common in the islands, and is the characteristic by which it is most commonly known.

As is well known this owl nests on the ground among the thick grass, and lays from three to six roundish white eggs.

Description.—Adult. General color from tawny ochraceus to buffy white, plentifully striped with dark drown; legs and under tail-coverts unmarked; wings marked with dark brown and ochraceous, with dusky bands. Orbital rings black; eye-brows whitish; no apparent ear-tufts. Length 13.80-16.75.

FALCONIDÆ.   HAWK AND FALCON FAMILY.

Buteo solitarius, Peale. Io.

The io is the only representative of the hawk family in the Hawaiian islands, save the accidental marsh hawk, and the rare fish hawk, so far as definitely known. The bird occurs only in the island of Hawaii, where it is generally diffused.. That a bird, possessed of such strong powers of flight as io, should be limited to a single island is most surprising and, indeed, unaccountable. Even, however, if the hawk reported from Kauai by Mr. Dole was of this species, the bird must be very rare upon that island, since no recent collector has obtained, or even seen it.

Upon both the windward and leeward sides of Hawaii the io is by no means a rare bird, though it is nothing like so common as it used to be in the old days. Inspired with the idea that any and all hawks must, from their very nature, destroy chickens, the settlers, for several years, have shot all hawks upon sight. This ruthlessness is all the more to be regretted since io rarely ever touches a chicken or, indeed, a native bird of any kind. I have made constant inquiry among poultry raisers in the heart of the io range, and have yet to find any one who has ever seen a hawk seize a chicken. The hawks have been suspected because they have been seen near the poultry-yard. As a matter of fact mongoose and rats, more especially the latter, are responsible for most of the depredations for which io is blamed. I have dissected more than thirty adult hawks collected upon the windward side of Hawaii, and have yet to find the first evidence of the chicken-eating propensities alleged against the bird. I have found as many as four mice in the crop and stomach of a single bird, and nearly every hawk examined had the remains of at least one mouse or rat. In the stomach of but two individuals have I found native birds. One of these had killed two akakanis and the other had killed an amakihi.

I have elsewhere noted the finding of the fragment of an egg— perhaps of the omao—in the stomach of one of these hawks which the bird had taken, presumably from the nest. I regret to be compelled to add that this is not the sole instance of the bird's propensity to rob nests which has come to my notice. I learn from an informant in Kaiwiki that he has seen hawks more than once in the very act of robbing mynahs' nests, despite the vociferous protests of a whole colony of the parent birds. The mynahs in this case had their nests in the forks of the main branches of some ohia trees close to the house. The hawks flew up against the

6–H B

trunks, maintaining themselves in this awkward position by means of their claws and their outstretched wings, and deliberately seized a young one and bore it off, repeating their predatory visits several times and in successive years.

Yet notwithstanding the fact that io sometimes destroys birds and may even occasionally seize a chicken, it is nevertheless apparent that the chief food of io, and, when he can get them, the only food, are mice and rats. When these are not to be had io contents himself with what he can find, among other things the larvae of the Sphinx moth and spiders. I have found the crops and stomachs of a number of individuals absolutely crammed with spiders. Large spiders of an introduced species (*Argiope avara*) have increased rapidly within the last few years, and it is but recently, apparently, that io has learned their value as food. The feathers of the legs and thighs of several hawks I have examined have been completely gummed up with a viscid secretion from the spiders and with the silken webs.

In view of the above facts it is a little difficult to understand the statements of some of the early explorers like Peale regarding this hawk, to the effect that "small birds constitute its principal food." The bird is large and sluggish and, though powerful of wing, possesses none of the rapidity of movement and alertness common to all bird-catching falcons. Io knows his business far too well to waste his time and strength in the vain pursuit of birds. When hungry he sits motionless upon the low limbs of trees watching for small rats, mice and other creeping things which he can pounce upon unawares.

Io shuns the dense forest—where alone most of the Hawaiian birds dwell—and lives upon its edges, especially where he has access to large cleared areas like cane and coffee fields. Both these are favorite hunting grounds, and he does excellent service in ridding the land of the above rodents which, as is well known, destroy both cane and coffee, to say nothing of corn and other farm products. Upon the whole Hawaii has no bird more important economically than this hawk, no bird perhaps which the agriculturalist cannot better spare. While there is yet time to preserve the species from extinction, laws should be passed protecting this hawk and imposing a heavy penalty for its destruction.

Like its American relatives of the genus *Buteo,* io is fond of soaring high in air in fine weather, especially towards midday, and once above the forest trees the bird mounts upward in wide spirals without perceptible movement of the wings until he is almost lost to sight in the blue ether. Under ordinary circumstances the flight of this hawk is heavy and labored, and is maintained at first by a series of rapid-wing-beats until the bird has secured good headway.

An instance has recently come to my notice where a hawk, undoubtedly of this species, accompanied a vessel all the way to California, most of the time perched on the royal yards. From this lofty perch, whence it could survey the ocean for miles around, it occasionally sallied forth after food which consisted of small birds, doubtless petrels.

The plumages of this hawk have not been well understood.* There is an extraordinary amount of individual variation, and in a series of over twenty specimens no two are alike. There are, however, but two distinct types or phases of the adult plumage, a very dark phase, in which the bird at a short distance appears to be black, and a light phase, in which the bird seems to be almost white. The juvenile plumage of each of these phases is very distinct from each other and from the corresponding adult condition; both of them, however, I believe have been described by authors as adult plumages. Juvenile specimens in the dark phase are very dark brown, but by no means so dark as the adult; those of the light phase are of a light brown type. Juveniles of both phases are, I think, several years in acquiring the adult plumage. The brown stripes and bars underneath are gradually replaced with buff in the light phase, and in the dark phase deepen and finally overspread the entire under surface.

The light and dark phases appear to mate in every possible combination, pairs of dark birds, pairs of white birds, pairs with both phases represented.

Dark birds are very much more numerous, at least on the wind-

*For a paper upon this subject by the author see "Ibis" for 1902.

ward sides of Hawaii, than light ones. I believe that not more than twenty-five per cent of the hawks on this side of the island are of the light phase.

Description.—Adult. Dark phase: Above and below blackish brown; feathers on throat and sides of head edged with rusty; rectrices with seven or eight zigzag black bars; interspaces ashy brown; inner webs of quills and secondaries white, barred with blackish brown. Legs greenish yellow; bill bluish black, plumbeus at base of lower mandible; eyris dark hazel.

The juvenile plumage of this phase is blackish brown above (though not so black as in adult); feathers of head and occiput edged with buff; chin, throat and breast buff deepening on sides, belly and tibiae into ochraceus, the feather of these parts with terminal shaft-streaks of dusky brown; belly and sides streaked with blackish brown; thighs and tibiae barred with same; tail and wings much as in adult.

Adult. Light phase: Head and hind neck light buff, streaked with dark brown; rest of upper parts dark brown; the upper tail-coverts washed with buffy the tertiaries and wing-coverts edged with buff and white; tail ashy brown with more or less distinct dark brown bearings. Under parts buff, deepest on belly and thighs, with a few indistinct brown shaft-streaks on sides. Eyris light hazel.

The juvenile plumage of this phase is dusky brown above, feathers, head, hind neck, sides of neck and wing-coverts with buff margins; under parts white with strong buffy tinge on sides of body where streaked with brown; thighs and tibiae barred with same; eyris light hazel.

Length of adult male, about 15½ inches; of adult female, about 18 inches.

Circus hudsonius (Linn.). Marsh Hawk.

I am not aware that there is any direct evidence of the occurrence of this species outside of Oahu, where several specimens have been obtained at different times. Nevertheless a recent visit to Oahu and much inquiry among sportsmen and others leads the writer to think that the specimens above alluded to were but casual visitors, and that the marsh hawk is not now, and never has been, a regular resident of the island.

Dole's *Accipiter Hawaii* is simply the *Buteo solitarius* as is shown under the heading of the following bird.

It is to be remembered that the marsh hawk would prove a welcome resident of the islands, especially of Hawaii, in which island there are immense tracts where this hawk should thrive and multiply. As the bird is a most indefatigable destroyer of mice and small rats it would prove an efficient ally of io in its war upon these pests.

Description.—Adult male. Upper parts, including head, neck and chest light bluish grey; upper tail-coverts white; tail bluish grey with white spots towards base, tipped narrowly with white, and with from five to seven dusky bands; lower parts sprinkled with brown.

Adult female. Above dusky brown, streaked and spotted with rusty; upper tail-coverts white; tail brown, banded with black; lower parts generally dull buff. Length 19-24 inches.

Pandion haliaëtus carolinensis (Gmelin). American Osprey.

It is difficult to state the precise nature of the occurrence of the osprey in the Hawaiian Islands. Mr. Perkins writes me that he has shot the bird upon Oahu, where it "is found as a straggler and no doubt at times on all the islands. It is, I believe, more frequent on Kauai and Niihau." The writer has neither seen nor heard of the osprey on Hawaii and, though the bird may occur here casually, the coast being well adapted to its habits, it is certainly neither a regular inhabitant nor a regular visitor to the windward side of the island.

The osprey seems to have been noticed long ago in the islands by Mr. Dole, though the fact has escaped the attention of recent writers. His notes (Hawaiian Annual, 1879, p. 42) under the heading of Pandion Solitarius, partly apply to this bird though the bird described is *Buteo solitarius.* He calls it "Osprey or Fish Hawk," gives its habitat as Hawaii, Molokai and Niihau, and adds the significant note that "it is probable that this bird inhabits all the Hawaiian Islands, *but as it frequents the most inaccessible coasts it is rarely noticed."* The above in nowise applies to the *Buteo solitarius* while entirely consonant with the view that the osprey was the bird in mind.

But the error does not stop here. Dole's *Accipiter hawaii* is quoted by Wilson in his "Birds of the Hawaiian Islands" as a synonym under *Circus hudsonius.* This citation I believe to be an error. Dole's *Accipiter hawaii*, as the description proves, is a young male *Buteo solitarius* in the brown phase of plumage.

This hawk was supposed by Mr. Dole to be an undescribed

species, its habitat being "Hawaii, rare on the rest of the group," and the type being a "mounted specimen in Mills' collection, Hilo, Hawaii. So far as I am aware the marsh hawk has never been found on the island of Hawaii and assuredly is not found there as a regular inhabitant. Moreover Dole's description, giving the length of his bird as 14 inches at once shows that the bird cannot have been a marsh hawk, if indeed the native name io given was not sufficient to show this. In further confirmation of the fact that Dole's bird cannot have been a marsh hawk, Mr. Brigham writes me that all the hawks from the Mills' collection in the Bishop Museum are io. As is well known all of the Mills' collection was acquired by the Bishop Museum, and there is little doubt that the particular specimen which served as Dole's type of *Accipiter hawaii* is among them though apparently unmarked.

It would seem certain that Mr. Dole as above cited had in mind two distinct species of hawks, and but two, neither of which was the marsh hawk. The two formal descriptions given apply to but one species, viz: *Buteo solitarius,* of which two phases of plumage are described, while the notes refer in part to that species and in part to the osprey.

There is little doubt that the osprey found in the islands is the American form, though specimens are necessary to finally settle the question.

Description.—Adult male. Above grayish brown; tail tipped with white, and with about six dusky bars; head, neck and under parts white; chest occasionally blotched with brown.

Female similar, but breast more heavily marked with brown. Length from about 21 to 25 inches.

APHRIZIDÆ   SURF-BIRD FAMILY.

Strepsilas interpres (Linn.).   Akekeke; Turnstone.

The akekeke occurs in great numbers throughout the archipelago, and in some localities is fully as numerous as the kolea. The two frequently associate, and by most sportsmen both are shot and eaten under the name of plover. It may be added that there is little difference to choose between the flesh of the two, and both are tidbits when in good order.

The first stragglers put in an appearance about the middle of August. In 1900 I shot some twenty of these first comers and to my great surprise found all of them to be plump and in fine order for the table, while some were very fat indeed. All these birds, with one exception, were fully adult and the majority were males. Moreover they were in much the same plumage as when they left for Alaska in May; that is, they were in the red and black plumage characteristic of the nuptial season. The young birds did not begin to appear till at least a fortnight later, and when they came were thin and poor.

The akekeke roost at night upon rocky points and little islets by the shore, where they are reasonably sure of being undisturbed and, about daybreak, leave for the pastures and freshly ploughed cane-fields where they feed all day. They and the plover destroy vast numbers of a small worm, called by the natives "pelua," which eats the freshly sprouted grass, and many other insects. On this account they are protected by some, but not all, the planters. Comparatively few akekeke remain in the islands all summer and, as stated elsewhere, these consist of the immature birds and the cripples. In some localities, however, the akekeke may be seen in large flocks all summer long, as near the crater of Kilauea, and many roost in the crater itself.

So far as I can learn the akekeke never has been known to breed in the islands.

Description.—Adult. Upper parts black and rufous; much white on head; rump, throat and belly white. Length 9-10 inches. Bill 8-9 inches. In juvenile dress the fufous is wanting; breast dusky.

CHARADRIIDÆ. PLOVER FAMILY.

Charadrius squatarola (Linn.) Black-bellied Plover.

The occurrence of this plover in the Hawaiian Islands rests, so far as the author knows, upon a single individual shot by Mr. George C. Hewitt in the fall of 1900 at Kaalualu, coast of Kau, Hawaii. That this is an isolated case is hardly to be believed, and it is more than likely that a few black-bellied plovers reach the islands every year in company with flocks of their relatives next mentioned.

Description.—Adult. Above blackish, variegated with white and yellowish; rump white with dark barring; below white, more or less shaded with grey; throat and breast with dusky spots. In summer under parts black; above variegated with black and white; tail barred with same; *a small hind toe.* Length about 12 inches.

Charadrius dominicus fulvus, (Gmelin.). Kolea; Pacific Golden Plover.

It must have been in very remote times that the kolea first discovered the Hawaiian Islands and established the habit of annually visiting their shores. No sooner have they reared their young in Alaska than they begin their return flight with its attendant dangers and fatigue. Leaving the islands in April and May, the first comers return about the middle of August. On that date of the present year (1900) I shot a number of kolea on the coast near Hilo in company with the akekeke above alluded to and, like the latter, they were all adults and had not yet doffed their nuptial dress, although beginning to moult. My friend, Mr. W. K. Andrews of Honomu, also reports that about the same time he saw numbers of first arrivals in the cane-fields near Honomu, and all were adults. It would seem, then that, directly the cares of the nesting season are over, the old males, and such of the females as have reared their young, start upon the return trip, leaving the young birds to be convoyed much later by the bulk of the females and a certain proportion of the males. Such, at least, may be inferred from the above notes, although many more observations will be necessary before all the facts concerning the migration of the kolea can be considered established.

As was the case with the akekeke, the kolea first to arrive were in excellent condition. In fact most of them were so fat that difficulty was experienced in preserving a specimen or two. Many observers have noted the fine condition the kolea are in just prior to the spring flight northward, but it seems remarkable that they should be able to make the long flight they are credited with *twice,* and in the interim raise their young, and still retain their plumpness. The young birds, unlike the old, seem to be invariably poor when they reach the islands.

Mr. Henry Patten of Hakalau has witnessed the actual arrival of some of these flocks upon Hawaii. When first they make the land they are evidently spent and weary by their long flight but soon measurably recover and begin to feed.

All the kolea do not arrive in the islands in great flocks at a given date, but the migration continues for a long time, more or less intermittently, from about the middle of August until at least November 1, at which late date flocks have been observed from shipboard nearing the islands. There would thus seem to be no concerted action in the fall migration. Flocks, large or small, just as it happens, take flight for the islands as the whim seizes them or, as is more likely, when they are in the proper condition for the trip.

There is every reason for believing that many of the migrants are lost in the long passage, especially in the late Fall, when so large a proportion of them are younglings, not yet seasoned to such prolonged flights. Small flocks of them are frequently encountered by vessels nearing the islands, and they usually act as though confused and uncertain as to their proper course, flying wildly about the vessel and uttering their calls as though quite bewildered.

The food of the kolea, while in the islands, is almost wholly obtained from the pastures and cane lands, especially from newly ploughed land, and consists chiefly, if not wholly, of worms and insects. The crops of some of those examined by me have been filled with insect remains, unfortunately in too fragmentary condition to enable their identity to be determined. It is highly probable that the kolea destroys a greater or less number of the beetle of the cane borer and, in any event, the number of insects it destroys is so great that the bird should be carefully protected by the plantation owners. No effort should be spared to encourage its presence in the cane fields with the hope that finally the bird may

*Observations made Sept. 9, 1901, corroborate the above. A number of kolea were shot at that date and all were adult but the moult into winter dress at this date was well towards completion.

be induced to breed in the islands and so remain the year round to wage war on insect pests.

In this connection I regret to be compelled to state that this fine bird is becoming scarcer and scarcer with every succeeding year. The fact that it visits all the islands in great numbers, added to the excellence of its flesh for the table, has long made it the favorite object of pursuit by island sportsmen and, as the latter have materially increased in numbers of late years, the plover have correspondingly diminished.

Neither the kolea nor the akekeke can go long without slaking their thirst, and from the barren uplands of Kau great numbers every day wend their way to the rare watering places which here are on the coast just above high water mark. The moment thirst is quenched the birds return to the feeding-grounds. These daily flights of the plover and akekeke after water afford the sportsmen their opportunity, and great numbers of the birds are killed from blinds placed within easy range of the watering places.

A comparatively small number of kolea roost upon the coast with the akekeke. By far the greater number assemble at nightfall and fly in flocks to one of the lava-flows which are so bare and inaccessible as to offer safe refuge from all enemies that have not wings. The floor of the crater of Kilauea also used to harbor thousands every night.

The first rains in the dry districts send the green grass above ground, and the plover soon become very fat feeding upon the worms and insects which infest the grass. By April all the kolea, both old and young, are in prime condition, having moulted and the old birds having now assumed in great part the dress of black and gold their wedding season calls for. During this month they leave the islands in large flocks, and by early May there are comparatively few left. Mr. Hoswell, of the Pepeekeo Plantation, Hawaii, informs me that in the early morning of the first days of April of the year 1900 he saw large flocks of kolea (and probably of akekeke) circling high in air over the coast and finally, after soaring in wide circles till almost out of sight, they took a northerly course and soon disappeared in the distance. Some of the flocks soared so high that they were lost to sight before settling upon their course. Doubtless these preliminary aerial evolutions are for the purpose of settling their course and, perhaps, of getting into favorable air currents. These migrating flocks have been sighted by the captains of more than one vessel at various points between San Francisco and the islands, and, as in Spring they are always steering north, there seems to be no reason to doubt that they are making direct for the Alaskan tundras.

Careful observations by sea captains upon these migrating flocks, giving the dates when the observations are made, the latitude and longitude in which the flocks are seen, and the course taken by them will still prove of great value, and will do much to assist in solving the somewhat mysterious and always interesting problems of bird-migration.

Description.—Adult. In summer above black, spotted with white and golden yellow; below black, but forehead, sides of head, neck and chest white. In winter no black below; belly white; chest and sides of neck washed with yellowish, and streaked with brown; upper parts spotted with greyish and gold; *no hind toe.* Length about 8 or 9 inches.

SCOLOPACIDÆ. SNIPE FAMILY.

Numenius tahitiensis (Gmelin). Kioea; Bristle-thighed Curlew.

The kioea appears to occur in small numbers upon all the islands, where it is chiefly a winter visitant. Upon the windward side of Hawaii the bird appears to be rather rare but Mr. Patten informs me that nearly every season he sees a few, usually a small flock, near Hakalau. Upon the Kau and Kona coasts the kioea is more common, and a certain number are shot there each year.

I feel sure that a large majority of these curlew make their appearance in September and October, and I have little doubt that they come from Alaskan breeding grounds with the kolea and the akekeke. Yet I am not prepared to assert that the kioea does not, at least occasionally, nest upon the islands. At Kaalualu, on the coast of Kau, where I saw a small flock of curlew the last of October, I was assured by Mr. Sam Kauhane that a few actually remain all summer, and he believed that some nested.

Mr. Wilson states that he, also, was told by natives that the kioea breeds in the islands. There can be no doubt that a few remain all summer, but this fact by no means gives positive assurance that they breed. Both the kolea and akekeke leave a contingent in the islands when they go north to nest in Spring but none of the stay-behinds have been known to breed. The curlew that remain all summer doubtless consist for the most part, as the kolea and akekeke certainly do, of the young birds, too immature to breed, and the old and the cripples. For all that, it is difficult to understand why the curlew and the other migrating species do not, in the course of time, settle permanently in the islands, where there would seem to be all the requisites.

Description.—Adult. Above dusky brown varied with buff; upper tail-coverts and tail ochraceous, the latter barred with dark brown; top of head dark brown with a medium stripe of buff; beneath dull buff; cheeks, neck and chest with brown streakings; side barred with same; thigh feathers with bristle-like points. Length about 17.25; the curved bill from 2.70 to 3.70.

Heteractitis incanus (Gmelin.).　Ulili; Wandering Tatler.

The ulili is a permanent inhabitant of the Hawaiian Islands, frequenting the rocky shores of all the members of the group as, indeed, it does of the Pacific islands generally. Solitary or in pairs its ringing note may be heard summer and winter as, disturbed, it flits from rock to rock. It feeds upon minute crustacea and small crabs and to obtain these follows the receding waves with nimble steps, running quickly back to avoid the incoming rush. It also follows the fresh-water streams a mile or two from the sea, and I have seen them feeding in pastures by the side of little rivulets. Nevertheless the sea-side is their proper home and they do not go far beyond the sound of its breakers.

Apparently the ulili never nests in the islands and, about April or May, the greater number accompany the plover in their northern flight. Before they depart many of the outgoing ulili assume the barred plumage which is characteristic of the nuptial season. While most go, many remain, the latter being the immature birds and the weaklings. At all events those that remain retain the immature or winter dress and show not the slightest inclination to breed.

About the middle or the latter part of August the return

migrants begin to appear, and it is noticeable that the first comers are adults, chiefly males and still in the nuptial dress which, however, is now somewhat worn and faded. Very soon after their arrival they begin the fall moult, and by the middle of September individual birds are to be found that show but a few barred feathers and have nearly donned the full winter suit.

The ulili does not appear to return to the islands in flocks but to drop in a few at a time, perhaps in flocks of other birds, as kolea and akekeke, and it is probable that the migration of the species is not concluded till early winter.

Description.—Adult. Above plumbeus grey; below white, streaked and barred with dusky. Length about 11 inches. In winter underparts are unspotted; breast plumbeus grey.

Limosa lapponica baueri (Naum.). Pacific Godwit.

According to Bryan a specimen of this godwit was secured by Mr. Francis Gay on the island of Kauai, while a fine specimen in winter dress is in the cabinet of Saint Louis College, Honolulu.

Mr. Rothschild notes (Avifauna of Laysan pt. 111, 307) that several were procured on Laysan Island by Prof. Schauinsland in May, 1896, which completes the present record for the islands.

The bird is found both on the Asiatic and Alaskan coasts, migrating as far south in winter as Australia and New Zealand.

Description.—Adult. Head, neck and lower parts cinnamon; back and scapularies irregularly varied with blackish, whitish and light rusty; wing coverts light greyish with dusky shaft-streaks and whitish margins. In winter head, neck and lower parts whitish; head and neck streaked, the back and sides irregularly barred with greyish brown; back and scapulars brownish grey. Length about 14.60-16 inches. (Ridgway.)

Calidris arenaria (Linn.). Hunakai; Sanderling.

Mr. Knudsen appears to have been the first to observe this species in the islands, and he secured several examples upon Kauai. In October of 1899 I secured two specimens at Kaalualu on the Kau coast. At this place the bird seems to be by no means rare and, although the natives did not know it by name, they assured me that it came in small numbers every year with the kolea and akekeke. Early in October of 1900 I saw two hunakai on the Hilo beach, where they made themselves very much at home, remaining there for at least a fortnight. Mr. Hewitt has sent me a third specimen which he shot at Kaalulalu October 14, 1900. September 25, 1901, I saw a little company of four on the Hilo beach. I am inclined now, therefore, to regard the hunakai as a regular migrant to the Hawaiian Islands, coming each year in small numbers which are likely to increase as time goes on.

Description.—Adult in winter plumage. Above pale grey, the feathers of head, back and rump with black central areas; hind neck and rump lighter; under parts pure white; bill and feet black. Length 7-8.75; bill about an inch.

Tringa acuminata (Hors.) Sharp-tailed Sandpiper.

One specimen was procured on Laysan by Professor Schauinsland and is now in the Bremen Museum. A second specimen was taken by Mr. A. F. Judd in Moanalua valley near Honolulu, and a third by Brother Matthias on Maui as recorded by Mr. Bryan in the Key. As this sandpiper is a common summer resident of Alaska, occasional individuals may be looked for in the islands accompanying the plover and akekeke in the Fall migration.

Description —Adult in winter plumage. Above grayish brown, streaked and striped with dusky; supercilliary stripe and lower parts dull white; chest and sides, breast, pale grayish buff. In summer the upper parts are brighter with rusty and black; unders streaked with dusky, and with greyish-brown V-shaped marks. Length about 8.25.

Tringa maculata Vieill. Pectoral Sandpiper.

Two specimens of this sandpiper have been shot by Mr. George C. Hewitt, one on the coast of Kau, Hawaii, the other a few miles inland, in the Fall of 1900. Both specimens were sent to me for examination.

Description.—Above brownish buff much marked with black; breast buff, with dusky streaks; rest of lower parts white. Length about 8.75.

Gallinago delicata (Ord). Wilson's Snipe.

One of these snipe was killed by Mr. Hewitt near Naalehu a

few years ago, as recorded in "The Auk" for July, 1900. In the Fall of the same year a second indivudual was seen in the same locality by Mr. W. H. Hayselden who, however, failed to secure it.

Description.—Adult. Above blackish, feathers edged with buff; below white; under wing-coverts, axillars and sides barred with slate. Length about 11 inches; bill 2.75.

RECURVIROSTRIDÆ. STILT FAMILY.

Himantopus knudseni, Stejneger. Kukuluaeo; Knudsen's Stilt.

This stilt was first described from specimens obtained in Kauai by the late Mr. Knudsen, although the birds' presence in the islands had long before been recorded by Pelzeln in 1873. Mr. Wilson obtained specimens in Oahu and Dr. O. Finsch observed it in Maui. There is, therefore, some reason to believe that the bird is distributed throughout the whole group. I have never seen it, however, upon Hawaii, nor have I been able to learn of its presence there. The aeo frequents the beach and also inland ponds and swamps. Upon Oahu, where but a few years ago the bird was numerous, it is now very scarce, having been mercilessly shot by gunners, though its flesh is of no value for food.

Description.—Adult. Above black; a small spot of white above and posterior to eye which is nearly encircled also with white; under parts white which color extends along side of neck and over the forehead in a broad band; tail smoky gray; legs bright pink.

PHALAROPIDÆ. PHALAROPE FAMILY.

Crymophilus fulicarius (Linn.). Red Phalarope.

A specimen of this phalarope was presented to the writer by Mr. M. Newell (Brother Matthias) who obtained it upon Kauai in the spring of 1894, where it appeared not to be uncommon. In April 1900 I shot a single individual from a flock of akekeke. How close was the association of this bird with the akekeke appears from the fact that it evidently accompanied the akekeke in the flight to the uplands to feed, quite contrary to the usual habits of this species which is pre-eminently a marine bird. Professor

Schauinsland saw this species upon the island of Laysan. It may be found that, like the sanderling, this phalarope visits the islands annually in small numbers.

Description.—Adult. Underneath purplish cinnamon; sides of head white; top of head blackish. In winter under parts white; occiput and about eyes plumbeous. Above pearl gray. Length 7.50-9 inches.

Phalaropus lobatus (Linn.).　Northern Phalarope.

So far as known, only a single specimen of this phalarope has ever been found on the islands. This individual was shot by Mr. A. F. Judd on Kauai during the winter of 1892-93, and is now in the Bishop Museum. The bird summers in Alaska, and migrated in great numbers down the west coast, so that occasional strays are to be looked for in the islands.

Description.—Adult. Above dark plumbeous, the back striped with buff; greater wing-coverts tipped with white; lower parts white; chest and sides rufous. The female much brighter than the male.

In winter chiefly white; upper parts grayish. Length about 7 inches.

RALLIDÆ.　RAIL AND MUD-HEN FAMILY.

Pennula millsi, Dole.　Moho.

There is a popular impression that this bird was wingless. As a matter of fact the moho was as well supplied with wings as most of the rail family, though it may be doubted if its wings were of any special use to it after it reached the islands. Obtaining its food solely from among the weeds and grasses, having no migration to perform, and at first having practically no enemies to escape from, the wings of the moho doubtless in time came to be almost useless. Nor would serviceable wings have long availed to preserve a bird of its secretive habits from the enemies destined to work its extermination, the domestic dog and cat (especially the latter) run wild in the islands. These wild cats have abounded in the woods from an early day, living upon rats, mice, and such young birds as chance throws in their way. The mongoose usually receives the credit of exterminating the moho, but it may be doubted if a single moho was alive at the comparatively late day when the mongoose came upon the scene. So far as the bird is concerned the matter is of no consequence since either enemy, cat or mongoose, was, unaided, quite capable of compassing its destruction.

Of the range and the habits of the moho we know very little. I am inclined to believe that forty or fifty years ago the moho ranged over a considerable portion of the windward side of the island, but not far above the sea.

The late Judge Austin told me that years ago it was not uncommon as far north along the coast as Onomea, and that on one occasion a native showed him a moho's nest with eggs, which was built in the grass close to a cane field. The late D. H. Hitchcock also informed me that less than forty years ago the moho lived on the edge of the woods not far above the town of Hilo, and that a nest with eggs was shown to him *in situ* by some boys. Thus it would appear that the moho ranged from somewhere near the volcano northward for forty miles or so along the coast and, perhaps, much farther. That the moho ever inhabited the dense woods of Olaa, as I find many people believe, is in the last degree doubtful. Mr. Mills' specimens, it is true, are supposed to have come from Olaa though their exact locality is unknown. Mr. Wilson states that Hawelu, the native who collected them, lived at the former half-way house on the old Volcano trail, and it was probably in the rather open country that here interposes between the woods and the sea that the moho lived.

A report is current in Hilo that when the Volcano road was being finished (about 1893) a moho was seen close to the road and some five miles east of the Volcano House. I have not been able to verify this report which, if true, brings the existence of the bird down to recent times, but the locality indicated is of all others the one in which I should expect to find this rail. The pahoehoe at this point is covered with a dense matting of mosses, lichens and ferns, above which rises in clumps a scattering growth of scrub, consisting of small ohias, berry-bearing trees, large ferns, vaccinium, ukiuki and many others. Even in dry weather the region is boggy and in wet weather it is a morass. Such a locality may well have been the last stronghold of the moho. In 1887 Mr. Wil-

7-H B

son searched the above region for the bird, and I have visited it many times since, but to no purpose. To explore this region thoroughly, however, with a dog would require weeks of persistent effort and would prove a most tremendous task.

What between the uneven and boggy nature of the ground, the presence on all sides of holes in the lava dangerous to limb if not to life, and the heavy growth over all which renders walking almost as difficult as through deep snow, the difficulties of exploration are of no ordinary kind. But more disheartening to the naturalist than all else is the presence of the mongoose which is there, as it is everywhere on the island, in force, and seems to render the quest for the moho at this late day an absolutely hopeless one.

Description.—Adult. Above rufous, lighter on head; side of head, chin, and throat whitish; beneath lighter rufous. Length about 5½ inches.

Pennula sandwichensis (Gmelin).

There is but one known specimen of this rail, that in the Leyden museum. I follow Sharpe and Rothschild in recognizing this specimen as the type of Latham's species, but it appears by no means certain that the specimen in question ever came from the Hawaiian Islands. To recognize a third species (*P. wilsoni*) is but to add to the existing doubt and confusion.

The following is a description of the Leyden specimen by Sharpe as quoted by Rothschild:

"Adult (type of species). General colour above ruddy brown with blackish centres to the feathers, producing a broadly striped appearance; wing-coverts like the back and very much elongated; quills blackish, with rusty-brown edges; tail-feathers blackish, completely hidden by the long feathers of the rump; head more uniform brown, with a ruddy tinge; sides of face like the head; throat and under surface of body dark vinous red, a little paler on the latter. Total length 5.3 inches, culmen 0.8, wing 2.8, tail 0.7, tarsus 1.3, middle toe and claw 1.35."

Porzanula palmeri, Froh. Laysan Crake.

This little rail is very abundant on the island of Laysan, where alone it is found, and amid its novel surroundings it has developed very remarkable habits. The following account is taken from Rothschild: Palmer says that it is "diurnal in its habits, very active, fearless and extremely inquisitive." Professor Schauinsland says of it: "This funny little rail has become accustomed to a totally new life; it lost its power of flight completely, and hardly uses its rudiments of wings to help it when running like a shadow across the sands with mouse-like speed. Originally more a swamp bird and dependent on worms, it has here become omnivorous, and the sea-birds must furnish its principal food. Although it cannot open their eggs with its thin beak, I have often seen it partake of the tasty inside of an egg when a *Telespiza* had broken one. It does not even despise corpses of birds, which are so frequent here, but it tears the flesh off in pieces and devours it; it feeds also chiefly on flies and the numerous beetles (*Dermestes*)."

"The nest of the Laysan crake is built under the thickest bunches of grass and there is a cover placed over it with a hole on the side for the bird to enter. It consists of grass woven together with very fine shreds of grass, fibres, and a little down, with here and there a feather intermixed, the materials softer inside."

"The eggs are longish oval and measure on an average 1.15 by 0.86 inch. The colour is pale creamy buff, flecked with pale reddish brown and pale purplish grey."

Description.—Adult. Above light brown, many of the feathers with blackish centers; sides of head and neck, chin, throat, breast and abdomen slaty gray. Bill light green; tarsus and feet greenish. Length about 6 inches.

Fulica alai, Peale. Alae keokeo.

In general appearance, habits, and notes this bird is the counterpart of the American fresh water coot from which, no doubt, it is descended, but from which it presents recognizable differences. The natives know it by the name of alae keokeo, white alae, in contradistinction from the red alae (Gallinula) because of its beautiful cream-colored frontal shieu (red in the Gallinule) and its white (faintly tinged with bluish) bill. The bird formerly figured prominently in Hawaiian folk-lore.

The alae is found upon all the islands and frequents shallow fresh water ponds, where there is an abundance of coarse reeds and sedges to serve for its own protection and to conceal its nest. When disturbed the birds instantly swim into the reedy recesses from which they can be dislodged only with the greatest difficulty. The nests are the same bulky piles of reeds and grasses character- istic of the coot everywhere. They are placed on the water, and are kept from floating away by the surrounding reeds. The birds begin to nest as early as the month of February and I have seen half-grown young freely swimming about in company with their parents April 30. Nesting thus early, the alae probably would be through with their domestic duties by mid-summer were it not for the fact that the natives freely plunder the nests for the eggs, which are excellent eating. In some localities it is only with great difficulty that the birds raise any young at all.

The only nest I ever saw, with anything in it, was found Aug- ust 17 and contained two fresh eggs, but I do not doubt that these were a second, perhaps even a third, laying. I have no means at hand of direct comparison, but I should judge it to be impossible to distinguish the eggs of the alae from those of the American species. The ground color is of a delicate creamy brown of the exact shade known as *cafe au lait,* numerously sprinkled with dots and roundish blotches of clove brown and purplish. They meas- ure: 188x130 and 144x125. The alae keokeo had achieved a rather conspicuous position in Hawaiian mythology, and had even risen to the dignity of a place in the Hawaiian pantheon, a fact which of itself indicates a residence in the islands of respectable antiquity.

Description.—Adult. Dark slate, paler below and much darker on head and neck; edge of wing, tip of secondaries and crissum white; legs and feet greenish gray; frontal knob delicate creamy white; bill faint bluish white. Length about 14 inches.

Gallinula galeata sandvicensis (Streets.). Alae ula. Hawaiian Gallinule.

The prominent place in Hawaiian mythology occupied by this

bird sufficiently attests the fact that it has been long a resident
of the islands. The alae ula is the bird that first stole fire from
the gods and gave it to the natives and, even to this day, it bears
upon its forehead the crimson frontal knob where the feathers were
burned away by the sacred fire.

The bird has overspread the islands and is found in the same
places as the coot. Unlike the latter bird, its nest is not placed
over the water where it is inacessible to the thieving mongoose.
The consequence is that in many localities upon the island of
Hawaii, as for instance, about Hilo, where formerly the gallinule
abounded, it is no longer known.

Dr. Stejneger has examined the claims of this bird to specific
rank with his usual acumen, and sums up the matter as follows:
"It seems, therefore, that there are no characters upon which to
base a specific separation, and were it not that the difference in regard to the color of the tarsus may hold good in the majority of
specimens, I should be disinclined to regard the Hawaiian bird as
even subspecifically distinct." I am not in position to add anything to Dr. Stejneger's remarks further than to say that the
single specimen of this bird I have been able to obtain near Hilo
had no trace of red upon the tarsus and, so far as I am able to see
without direct comparison with American specimens, is indistinguishable from ordinary American examples.

Description.—Adult. Head, neck and under parts grayish black, darker
on head and whitening on belly; back brownish olive; wings and tail
dusky; crissum, edge of wing and flanks white; bill, frontal plate and
tibiae anteriorly (usually) red; tarsus and toes greenish. Length 12-15
inches.

ARDEIDÆ. HERON FAMILY.

Ardea sacra, Gmelin. Aukuu.

According to Rothschild this heron has been ascribed to the
Hawaiian Islands by G. R. Gray, but without citation of authority.
Dole also gives it as an inhabitant of the group (Proc. Bost. Soc.
Nat. Hist. 1869, p. 303) but his statement that it is "common all
over the group" is assuredly a mistake, and tends to throw some
doubt upon the accuracy of his knowledge respecting the species.

Dr. Finsch, who was well acquainted with the bird in the islands further south, is quoted by Rothschild as stating that he "observed the white form once at Kahului, Maui."

I can add no certain evidence of the occurrence of the bird in the islands, although a large white heron which I am informed was seen in Honolii gulch near Hilo, Hawaii, can hardly have been anything else except the white form of this species.

Description.—Adult, Above cinereous blue; abdomen dusky; plumes of back and breast white. Length about 17 inches. The young is wholly white.

Nycticorax nycticorax griseus (Bodd.). Aukuu kahili; Black-crowned Night Heron.

This heron is numerous on Oahu, and even about Honolulu, being found on the Nuuanu stream quite within the city limits. It is common also upon Maui, and occurs on all the other islands in greater or less numbers. Upon Hawaii it is comparatively rare, at least upon the windward side, though I have seen a number about the Lokoaka ponds, not far from Hilo. Formerly it was occasionally found on the Waiakea ponds close to Hilo, and I have heard of a number being seen on the upper Wailuku close to the forest.

The habits of the bird during its residence on the islands appear to have undergone no change. Usually the herons roost by day in the lauhalas, mangoes and other trees of dense growth and, about dusk, betake themselves to feed in the shallow brackish and fresh-water ponds, their chief prey being oopu and other allied small fish.

Upon Oahu a considerable number of these herons are killed by the Portuguese under the name of "fish-hawks" and eaten, and their rank flesh is highly esteemed.

Description.—Adult. General color bluish gray; crown, scapulars and interscapulars dark glossy green; forehead, throat and underparts generally whitish; occipital plumes white. Length about 24 inches.

Young birds lack the plume, and are otherwise very different. Above, grayish brown, paler below; much spotted with white.

IBIDÆ. IBIS FAMILY.

Plegadis guarauna (Linn.). Glossy Ibis.

The occurrence of this ibis in the Hawaiian Islands has hitherto rested upon a single specimen obtained by Mr. Knudsen in 1872, upon Kauai, and identified by Mr. Ridgway as of the above species. Mr. Newell informs me that in 1873 Mr. Wilder of Honolulu shot a second specimen of this ibis on the island of Maui, and sent it to him for preparation. It was probably of the above species, though this is not definitely known.

Description.—Adult. Head, neck and lower parts chestnut; upper parts metallic green, bronze and purple; lores lake-red; feathers at base of bill white. Length about 22 inches.

Young with lower parts grayish brown.

ANATIDÆ. GOOSE, DUCK AND SWAN FAMILY.

Bernicla sandvicensis (Vigors). Nene. Hawaiian Goose.

The nene is now found chiefly, if not wholly, upon the island of Hawaii, although it is said to have nested in past times in the crater of Haleakala on the island of Maui and, occasionally, to have been seen on the islands of Kauai and Niihau. At the present time, however, there is no reason to believe that the nene is found upon Maui, inquiry in 1891 failing to disclose that it has been seen there for several years. Its occurrence upon Kauai and Niihau was probably in the nature of an accident, if indeed it was not mistaken for one of the species of American geese which are now known to visit the islands not rarely.

Upon the island of Hawaii the haunts of the nene, for the greater part of the year, are the uplands from about 5,000 feet upwards. At or about the above elevation the range of this goose is quite extensive, and it is found from the district of Kona to the northeast flanks of Mauna Kea. It would be an easy matter to introduce the nene from Hawaii into the other islands, especially Maui, and no doubt the bird would thrive, if properly protected.

The region it affects is open, and, in general, as barren as can well be imagined, consisting for the most part of lava flows, naked except for very scanty growth of ferns, ohelos, puakeawe, and a few other lowly shrubs. Except for the temporary rain-water pools this region is entirely devoid of water, and it is doubtful if this goose drinks, or indeed cares to drink, any other fluid than the ·dew it may find on the grasses and berries it eats. The bird has lived so long amid its novel surroundings that it has become entirely weaned from the habits of its kind, and never enters water, but is in all essential respects a land goose.

The food of the nene consists of pualele (*Sonchus oleraceus*), tender grasses and several kinds of berries, especially the ohelo (*Vaccinium reticulatum*), puakeawe (*Cyathores tameiameiae*), and the strawberry (*Fragaria chilensis*). In summer when the latter abound in the upper districts, the geese become very fat, and are then fine eating. The young birds, however, and the old ones too for that matter, are said to be more fond of the milky juiced weed called by the natives pualele than anything else, and to live largely upon it from their adolescent stage onwards.

When captured young the nene are rather difficult to rear, but if they live are readily domesticated, and eventually become excedingly tame, following their owner about and permitting themselves to be freely handled. A pair kept for several years by Mr. Walton of the Pahala plantation, Kau, were very playful and, when invited to a romp, would chase a lad round the enclosure with every manifestation of delight. In some districts I am told they breed rather freely in confinement, but such it not always the ·case. Numbers of these geese have been taken to England from time to time, where they have been successfully kept for years and, in some instances as I am assured have reared young.

That the mongoose, to some extent at least, have invaded the upland homes of this goose there is only too much reason to believe, and it remains to be seen if the bird can long maintain itself against the attacks of this fierce marauder. The barren flats near the sea where this goose nest would seem to be entirely unsuited to the mongoose, yet in riding over these flats looking for geese I saw mongoose, which doubtless are ever ready to plunder an unprotected nest or to seize an imprudent young one. A goose, however, with its nest to defend, or its young to protect, is no contemptible foe, and it is to be hoped that this fine bird may be able to hold its own in the contest.

The mongoose is not the only, nor the chief, foe the nene has to fear, since the districts frequented by the bird most of the year, though remote and inaccessible, are now often visited by sportsmen, and the nene is rapidly diminishing in numbers. The time will inevitably come, and that soon, when this goose will need protection from sportsmen to save it from its otherwise inevitable fate of extermination.

In this connection attention may well be called to the fact that, as the present law stands, the open months (from September 15 to February 1), when the killing of this goose is permissable, are almost precisely the ones in which it rears its young. The law, doubtless through a misapprehension of the facts, protects the bird when it least needs protection, and exposes it to slaughter when it is laying its eggs and leading about its young.

The breeding season of the nene is a very protracted one, as is that of all Hawaiian birds, and Mr. Eben Low informs us that some pairs begin to lay the latter part of August, and the nesting season is not all over and the young able to shift for themselves till April or even later. Thus the months that by law are now open ones should be closed, and the close time extended somewhat.

It has been stated and seems to be the general impression that the nene rears its young in the uplands where it is found in summer, but such is not the fact. The greater number, probably all, leave the upper grounds beginning early in the fall, and resort to lower altitudes, from about 1,200 feet downwards. There are barren lava flats near the sea in Puna, Kona, Kau and Kohala, rarely indeed visited by man, and it is to these deserted solitudes that the nene resorts at the beginning of the love season.

The cause of the desertion of the uplands by the geese for the low-lying lava flats near the sea is doubtless the failure of the food supply in the former, at least of such as is adapted to the wants of the young. At high altitudes there is but a scanty crop of berries in winter, and most of the pualele dies; whereas near the sea there is an abundance of this plant and of freshly sprouted grasses during the winter and spring months.

Mr. Eben Low informs me that the nene is much attached to its old nesting ground, and is wont to return season after season to the same locality to deposit its eggs. This fact is well known to the natives who; when once they find a nest, never fail to return the following year to secure the young. It is when leading about their young that the old birds undergo the moult, and, when deprived of their wing feathers and unable to fly, they, and the young, are easily run down by the fleet-footed natives and secured.

Mr. Palmer Wood, of Kohala, who has several pairs of nene in confinement, tells me that they lay from three to six eggs, the former being doubtless the more usual number. The nest of a wild bird which he found in a lava flat was placed among low bushes, and was made by scraping the surrounding dirt into a hollow pile. The eggs are laid directly upon the earth, but finally are surrounded with down plucked from the breast of the old birds, after the usual manner of the *Anatidæ*. When the bird (tame or wild) temporarily leaves the nest, the down is carefully disposed over the eggs, probably for the double purpose of hiding them and keeping them warm.

Mr. Sam Kauhane also has found the nest of the wild bird on the lava below Kahuku, Kau. The eggs, in this instance four in number, were on the bare ground, but were encircled by a slight barrier of bits of brush.

Mr. George C. Hewitt, of Naalehu, has kindly presented the writer with two eggs, laid by one of his geese in confinement, and a third was presented by Mr. C. M. Walton of Pahala. These eggs are of a delicate creamy white (brown stained when long set on) and measure as follows: 3.37x2.42; 3.32x2.45 ;3.40x2.18.

Description.—Adult male. Hind neck, head, cheeks, chin and throat black, as also a narrow ring around lower throat; rest of neck and sides of head brownish buff; feathers on throat and sides of neck narrow and acute and so arranged as to disclose their black bases; above deep hoary brown, feathers margined broadly with brownish white; rump and tail dusky black, as also the primaries; beneath grayish brown; feathers on sides and flanks with gray tips; lower belly and under tail-coverts white; bill and feet black. Length 23 to 28 inches, the female the smaller.

The appearance of this handsome goose is much enhanced by the arrangement of the neck feathers. These are somewhat stiff and lanceolate, and are so disposed in oblique and more or less parallel rows as to disclose the black bases in the intervening furrows, thus producing a market and novel effect.

Branta nigricans (Lawrence). Black Brant.

"Palmer obtained a specimen of this bird from Brother Matthias, who got it at Kahului, on the island of Maui, in 1891." (Rothschild Avifauna of Laysan, pt. III, p. 279. 1900.)

Description.—Adult. Head and neck black; above dark drown; neck with broad white collar, interrupted behind; below dark sooty slate; crissum white; bill and feet black. Length from 22 to 23 inches.

Branta canadensis minima (Ridgway). Cackling Goose.

According to Rothschild Mr. Palmer shot a specimen of this goose, the only one known to have found its way to the islands, near Waimea, Kauai, March 16, 1891.

During the winter months of 1900-1901 two separate flocks of Canada geese made their appearance in Hilo bay, and remained for a considerable period. In all there were upwards of fifteen reported. A number, possibly all, were killed at one time and another, but as I was unable to obtain a sight of a single individual I am unable to state which form of the Canada goose was represented by these birds.

The above instances are not the only ones I have heard of, and I believe it is not a rare thing for geese to make their way to the islands in the fall and to winter here. Sooner or later, no doubt, all of the geese from the northwest coast will be recorded as casual winter visitors.

Description.—Adult. Head and neck black; a white patch on cheek; lower neck encircled by white collar; upper parts brownish, feathers with lighter tips; lower parts deep grayish brown; anal region white; bill and feet black. Length from 22 to 25 inches.

Chen hyperborea (Pall.). Lesser Snow Goose.

A single specimen of this goose was obtained on the island of Maui by Brother Matthias as recorded by Rothschild.

Description.—Adult. Uniform white; head usually stained with rusty; primaries black bill and feet purplish red. Length from 23 to 28 inches.

Young birds have grayish head, neck, and upper parts; rump, upper tail-coverts, tail and lower parts white.

Anser albifrons gambeli (Hartlaub). American White-fronted Goose.

A male of this goose was shot by Palmer at Honokohau, island of Hawaii, Dec. 18, 1891, as recorded by Rothschild.

Description.—Adult. Fore part of head to about half way across lores and forehead white; rest of head grayish brown, as also neck and upper parts; below grayish white, blotched with black; crissum and tail-coverts white; bill and feet yellowish or orange. Length 27 to 30 inches.

Dafila acuta (Linn.). Koloa mapu. Pin-tail Duck.

Well known to sportsmen as a winter visitor to the islands, where, some seasons, it seems to be rather numerous.

Description.—Adult male. Head and upper neck hair-brown, glossed with green and purple; sides of head with white stripe; dorsal line of neck black; lower neck and under parts white; back and sides vermiculated with black; speculum greenish purple; tertials and scapulars silvery and black; tail cuneate with much projecting middle feathers. Length about 28 inches.

Female. Above grayish dusky with bars and streaks of yellowish brown; lower parts chiefly white; flanks and under tail-coverts streaked with dusky. Smaller.

Spatula clypeata (Linn.). Koloa moha. Shoveller.

Well known to the island sportsmen as the "North-west duck." It winters in large numbers in the Hawaiian Islands, especially upon Oahu and Kauai, and occurs upon the island of Hawaii in flocks of considerable size. Capt. Wm. Matson informs me that when about 300 miles off the port of Hilo, October 31, 1900, he observed a flock of about fifty ducks, presumably of this species. They seemed to be lost, and followed the vessel for two days, practically into port. They kept lighting in the water near by, and when the vessel forged ahead a few miles they overtook her, circled around, and again alighted only to repeat the performance.

The flock seemed to have lost their bearings and to be following the vessel as a guide.

Description.—Adult male. Head and neck green; breast and outer scapulars white; rest of under parts chestnut; crissum dark bluish green, bordered anteriorly by white; bill black and twice as wide at tip as at base; feet orange-red. Length about 20 inches. Female duller.

Anas americana (Gmelin). Baldpate.

A single juvenile specimen of this duck was taken by Professor Schauinsland on Laysan, October 15, 1896. So far as I am aware this duck has not yet been found in the main group.

Description.—Adult male. Head and upper neck white, speckled with dusky; sides of head with brown patch of metallic green; sides and flanks vinaceous; back and scapulars grayish white. Female is duller. Length from 18 to 22 inches.

Anas boschas Linn. Mallard.

Professor Schauinsland obtained a single adult male of this species on the island of Laysan, July 11, 1895. This is the first and, so far as I know, the only record for the islands.

Description.—Adult male. Head and upper neck glossy green; neck encircled with a white ring; breast purplish chestnut; greater wing-coverts tipped with white and black; speculum violet with border of black; bill greenish yellow; feet orange red. Female with the wing as in the male; elsewhere mixed dusky and ochraceous. Length about 24 inches more or less.

Anas carolinensis Gmelin. Green-winged Teal.

This is another of the American ducks of which Prof. Schauinsland obtained a single specimen upon Laysan Island. This bird was obtained October 27, 1896.

Description.—Adult male. Head and upper neck chestnut with broad patch of green behind eye, bordered by white; a broad white bar across side of breast; upper hind neck with tuft of bluish black; chin and upper throat black; lower neck, upper back, scapulars, sides and flanks mixed black and white; speculum metallic green.

Adult female. Above grayish dusky with buffy edgings and bars; head.

neck and lower parts brownish white; head and neck streaked with dusky; sides and flanks with dusky spots; belly usually speckled with white. Length from 13 to 15 inches.

Anas wyvilliana, Schlater. Koloa.

The little native duck, or koloa as the natives call it, is widely spread over the archipelago, no island being without it. Upon the island of Hawaii the koloa used to be numerous, being by no means uncommon about Hilo, the type locality, as recently as five years ago. But as the mongoose has increased in numbers, the koloa has diminished, and it is no longer found immediately about Hilo at all, while it is becoming comparatively scarce in other parts of the island. I believe that generally speaking the bird is becoming less numerous upon all the islands, both because of the attacks of the mongoose and because it is more sought after by sportsmen than formerly.

The old birds of course are rarely killed by the mongoose, which never pursues its prey into the water, except when setting. As the koloa, like most other ducks, makes its nest upon the land the setting birds and their eggs must frequently fall easy prey to the keen nosed and fearless mongoose.

The koloa is a fresh water duck, although by no means entirely absent from the coast, and it loves to follow the windings of the little mountain stream as they thread their way through the tangled woods, here and there forming little pools of still water. It is in such localities, rather than near the coast, that this duck usually nests.

In localities where unharrassed the koloa is tame and unsuspicious, and its destruction is easily compassed by the sportsman.

In October of 1899 a pair of these ducks was shot at Kaalualu on the coast of Kau, Hawaii, by Mr. Bertelmann and presented to the writer. Upon dissection the stomachs of both birds were found to be crammed with two species of small fresh and brackish water shells. The larger of the two proves to be the *Melania newcombii* Lea which abounds in all the islands of the group. The smaller has been identified by Mr. C. F. Ancey as the *Hydrobia porrectamigh*.

Description.—Adult. Top of head blackish; neck, upper back and inter-scapulars brown with rufous brown bands; lower back, rump and upper tail-coverts brownish black; speculum deep purple, bordered with white; sides of head, neck and throat brown mottled; breast rufous brown with U-shaped blackish markings; abdomen brownish buff; sides of body rufous heavily marked with deep brown. Length about 20 inches.

Anas laysanensis, Rothschild. Laysan Teal.

This duck, which is even smaller than the preceding species, appears to be limited to the island of Laysan, where it is fairly numerous in the scrub. Though often seen on the beach, Palmer never observed this duck in the water, and it appears to have become as thoroughly habituated to a strictly land life as the nene, or Hawaiian goose.

This duck is a near relative of the preceding species, and evidently both are derived from the same stock.

Description.—Adult. Above deep blackish brown, darkest on rump and upper tail-coverts, with irregular U-shaped markings of light rusty-brown; crown black; an irregular ring of white about eye; speculum deep green, tipped with white; below pale rusty brown, irregularly barred and spotted. Length about 15 to 17 inches. Female smaller.

Merganser serrator (Linn.). Red-breasted Merganser.

This duck was recorded by me in the "Auk" for April, 1893, as a "casual and possibly a rather regular winter visitor" to the islands on the strength of two specimens shot near Hilo. No others have been seen since and, were it not for the fact that the bird seemed to be familiar to the natives to whom I showed the specimen I shot, I should be inclined to look upon its occurrence here as purely accidental. Mr. Bryan in his Key notes its occurrence on Oahu.

Description.—Adult. Head greenish black and crested; above pied black and white; rump, upper tail-coverts and tail ash gray; neck and sides of chest light cinnamon, streaked with black; lower parts white or salmon colored. Length 20 to 25 inches.

Charitonetta albeola (Stejneger). Buffle-head.

Mr. Bryan records a single specimen as being in the cabinet of

Saint Louis College, Honolulu. This specimen was obtained on the island of Maui by Brother Matthias. The bird is one of the commonest of the continental ducks.

Description.—Adult. Head and upper neck metallic green glossed with purple on the crown; back and upper parts black; a white patch from behind the eye across the occiput; lower neck, under parts, secondaries and scapulars white. Female duller. Length about 12.50 inches.

FREGATIDÆ. MAN-O'-WAR BIRD FAMILY.

Fregata aquila (Linn.). Iwa. Man-o'-War bird.

Apparently the iwa does not breed upon the Hawaiian group proper unless, perhaps, on Niihau. That it breeds in great numbers upon Laysan and the neighboring islands was ascertained by Palmer. The iwa is not infrequently seen about Oahu and even in Honolulu harbor. Knudsen obtained a single individual on the coast of Kauai. I have never observed the bird upon the windward side of Hawaii, nor has anyone else, so far as I can ascertain.

According to Rothschild the iwa breeds in rookeries of from half a dozen to fifty, building their nests on the scrub, and laying one white egg.

The iwa lives chiefly upon fish which they catch themselves, when so unfortunate as to be unable to find any other sea-bird which they can compel to disgorge its finny prey. They are aggressive thieves under all circumstances, and will steal the young of the gannet and other sea-birds in the very presence of the parents.

Description.—Adult male. Black all over with metallic gloss on scapulars and interscapulars. Female dull black; breast and sides whitish. Length about 40 inches.

Phalacrocorax pelagicus Pall. Pelagic Cormorant.

Mr. Rothschild records a single specimen of this cormorant from the island of Laysan where taken by Professor Schauinsland October 22, 1896. Late in November of 1900 two cormorants made their appearance in Hilo bay and remained till into the spring of 1901. One of them was shot, but what became of the other is unknown. It is possible that they were of the present species, or they may have been one of the other west coast forms that chanced to find their way here in company with the flocks of ducks that each fall wing their way to the islands for the purpose of wintering.

Description.—Adult. Head and neck violet black with changeable reflections; rest of body greenish. In breeding dress, neck and rump with white filamentous feathers; flanks marked with white. Juvenile birds of a dusky brown.

FAMILY SULIDÆ. THE GANNETS.

Sula cyanops (Sundev.). Masked Gannet.

But one of the gannets have been reported from the main group, though the others may be expected to occur in the contiguous waters, at least casually. The present species breeds both on Laysan and French Frigate Islands. No nest is made, but the two eggs are laid on the sand. All the members of the family live upon fish.

Description.—Adult. White; wing-coverts and alulae sooty brown; tail mostly sooty brown; feet yellowish. Length about 28 inches. The young are brown above, lower parts white.

Sula piscator (Linn.). Red-footed Booby.

Knudsen secured a specimen of this gannet on the coast of Kauai, concerning which he says: "The other day, when the men were out fishing, this bird came up to the canoe and tried to take the fish off their hooks." (Proc. U. S. Nat. Museum, Vol. XII, p. 383, 1890.)

This species is very plentiful on Laysan, as reported by Palmer, and was often seen, also, at sea. This and the following species both make nests upon bushes. The red-footed booby is said to lay but one egg. (Rothschild.)

Description.—Adult. White, head and neck with buffy tinge; remiges slate color; shafts of rectrices yellowish; feet yellowish. Length about 28 inches.

8–H B

The young are sooty brown above; head, neck and lower parts smoky gray.

.Sula sula (Linn.).   Booby.

According to Rothschild this gannet was very plentiful on Lisiansky and Midway Islands, and was noticed by Palmer off Niihau.   It is however, "altogether the rarest of the three species in these waters and was absent from Laysan."

"This species builds a nest of twigs on scrub and lays two eggs, but on Midway Island, where only grass is found, it builds on the ground.

Description.—Adult.   Mostly sooty brown; lower parts from breast backwards white.   Length 30 to 31 inches.

The young are sooty brown all over, but paler below.

PHAETHONTIDÆ.   TROPIC BIRD FAMILY.

Phaëthon lepturus Laup. V. Daudin.   Koae. Salmon-tailed Tropic Bird.   Bos'n.

In the "Auk" for January, 1901, the writer called attention to the presence of the "Yellow-billed Tropic Bird" on the coast of the island of Hawaii, giving it the name of *P. americanus*.   He was not aware at the time that the Pacific Ocean form of the yellow-bill had been described under the name *lepturus*.   Subsequently, through the kindness of Director Brigham, an opportunity was had to examine all the specimens of tropic birds in the Bishop Museum, when it appeared that but two species were represented, viz: *lepturus* and *rubricauda*.   In other words it became at once apparent that the bird which had been recorded from the coast of the several islands by various observers as *P. æthereus* was, in all probability, the present species.

Mr. Rothschild independently reached the same conclusion from the examination of the material in the Tring Museum, and the matter is duly set forth in part III, Avifauna of Laysan, p. 296.

The error of identification dates back as far as 1869 when Mr. Dole, in Proc. Bost. Soc. Nat. Hist. p. 308, gives *P. æthereus* as a resident of the islands without reference or comment.   There can

be no doubt that he, also, had in mind the present species. Thus
œthereus has no present claim whatever to be considered a bird
of the islands.

The koae, as the natives call this and the next species, is common along the windward side of Hawaii, frequenting, however,
only those portions of the coast where the presence of cliffs offers
cavities in which the birds may roost and nest.

On sunny days the bos'n is frequently to be seen as, singly or in
pairs, they slowly winnow their way along the cliffs, apparently
inspecting them with a view to the selection of future homes. At
such times the birds often fly over points of land that project into
the sea, and occasionally are seen even over the cane-fields chasing
each other in play.

Lepturus appears to be the only species that now lives upon the
windward side of Hawaii, although it is reasonable to suppose
that the following bird occurs here, at least occasionally.

For some reason or other this bird of late years is much less
numerous along the island of Hawaii than it used to be, and the
same is true of Oahu and, I believe, of all the other islands of the
group. The mongoose has been blamed for this decrease in the
numbers of the koae, but it must be only in very exceptional instances when this animal can reach their practically inaccessible
nests in the steep faces of the cliffs.

The long tail feathers of this and the following species were
formerly highly valued for decorative purposes as, also, were the
body feathers.

It is a common habit of this bird to visit the neighborhood of
its nest once or more during the daytime, either alone or in company with its mate. These visits by the birds seem to be for no
other purpose than to assure themselves that their home is all
right, and has not been molested during their absence. The birds
fly about the locality, now a mile out to sea then back again, for
an hour, more or less, occasionally setting the wings and darting
up to the very mouth of the cavity which shelters their young or
egg. I have thought that their object at such times might be to call
the young bird to the mouth of the burrow for the purpose of
feeding it. I have never been able, however, to catch sight of the

nestling nor, apparently, do the birds go close enough in to effect such a design, even could they accomplish it without making a perceptible pause.

Formerly this tropic bird frequented the steep banks of the Wailuku River, Hawaii, and nested three or four miles up that stream, but they no longer do so.

I believe this is the tropic bird that is often seen over the pit of Kilauea on fine sunny days and which breeds in the cliffs that limit the western side, although Mr. Wilson in his volume states that he shot the *P. rubricauda* there.

Description.—Adult. General color pure white, with distinct rosy tinge below; a black bar through eye; tertiaries mostly black; outer edge of primaries and shafts of tail feathers black; feathers of sides, flanks and upper tail-coverts with central streaks of black; two central tail feathers, projecting 8 or 9 inches beyond the rest, of a deep salmon color, sometimes in summer fading to nearly pure white; bill greenish yellow, indeterminately marked with bluish black; legs and feet pale bluish; webs black. Length 22-23 inches.

Phaëthon rubricauda (Bodd.). Koae. Red-tailed Tropic Bird.

The red-tail occurs probably off all the islands of the main group, although the writer feels by no means sure that Wilson has not confounded this and the preceding species when he states (Aves Hawaiiaensis) that "it breeds in several places in the group, especially on Kauai and Niihau, and choses holes in almost inaccessible cliffs wherein to deposit its eggs." These remarks certainly apply well to *lepturus,* and it may prove to be that species only which frequents the rocky cliffs of the main group. As noted by Wilson, the nesting habits of *rubricauda* on Laysan are very different since there, according to Palmer, "they make a hollow in the ground under the bushes for their nest."

The writer has not met with this species on the windward side of Hawaii, nor do any of the resident natives appear to be acquainted with it. He learns, however, that it has been seen and shot on the coasts of Hamakua and Kohala, on the northern extremity of the island.

Upon the island of Laysan this tropic bird nests in June. Both species lay but one egg.

Description.—Adult. General color satiny white with more or less of a rosy tinge; above barred and spotted with black; a black crescent before the eye and a smaller one behind; two central, elongated tail-feathers crimson with black shafts; bill red; feet yellowish; toes black. Length about 30 inches.

PROCELLARIIDÆ. PETREL FAMILY.

Puffinus cuneatus, Salvin. Wedge-tailed Puffin. Uau Kane.

This rare petrel was originally described by Salvin from the Krusenstern Islands (Marshall group), and the same year (1888) was redescribed by Stejneger as *P. knudseni* from Kauai from specimens furnished by Mr. Knudsen. Of the occurrence of the species on Kauai, Mr. Knudsen says: "It was formerly found plentiful every summer at the top of the mountains as high up as 5,000 feet, where they had their nests in long burrows, but that in the last ten years they have become rare, as the foreign rats kill them in their nests."

This puffin was observed by Palmer on all the northwestern islands except Midway, but only in small numbers. He says it "lives in pairs and lays only one egg in a rude nest made of grass in a burrow in the sand."

Description.—Adult. Above sooty brown, darker on head, rump and wing-coverts; quills and tail-feathers black; underparts white; sides of head and body gray; bill horn-gray; feet pink. Length about 17 inches.

Puffinus newelli, Henshaw. Newell's Puffin.*

This bird was first obtained by Mr. M. Newell on the island of Maui in the spring of 1894, several of them having been taken from their burrows by the natives and brought to Mr. Newell alive. Two specimens were saved, one of which, the type, is in my possession, the other being in the museum of St. Louis College in Honolulu.

---

*This species was described by the author in "The Auk" for July, 1900. By an unfortunate misprint it was ascribed to the island of "Ulani" instead of Maui.

At the time mentioned the species was numerous in the Waihee valley and probably elsewhere on Maui, but it is to be feared that the species has since suffered from the mongoose, which is rapidly exterminating the native puffins elsewhere on the islands. At present no particulars of its habits are known.

Mr. Bryan in his Key gives the island of Kauai also as the habitat of the species, where it was obtained by Mr. Francis Gay, and the bird may prove to be somewhat generally dispersed throughout the group. I saw numerous puffins in the channel between the islands of Molokai and Maui. They were rather close to the steamer, and their appearance seemed to exactly coincide with the present species.

Description.—Adult. Above, including upper surface of wings and tail, clear and somewhat glossy black. Border of under wing-coverts black. Beneath, including under tail-coverts, pure white. Maxilla and edge and tip of mandible black; rest of maxilla light brown. Tarsus and feet light yellow, but black along the outer posterior side of tarsus, the outer toe and half the middle toe. Wing, 8.65; tail, 3.75; bill, 1.28; tarsus, 1.80.

Puffinus nativitatis Streets. Christmas Island Shearwater.

Recorded by Mr. Bryan in his "Key to the Birds of the Hawaiian Group" as from the French Frigates and Laysan Islands.

Description.—Adult. Lower parts uniform dusky black; bill deep black; under wing-coverts deep sooty black; primaries and tail feathers black. Length about 15 inches.

Oceanodroma castro (Harcourt). Ake-Ake. Hawaiian Stormy Petrel.

Nothing appears to be known concerning the occurrence of this petrel in the islands, save that two specimens were collected by Mr. Knudsen on Kauai, from which the species was described by Mr. Ridgway, and that it has been observed and collected on Niihau by Mr. Gay. Mr. Rothschild notes the bird also from French Frigate Island.

I have little doubt that the akeake is much more common and widely dispersed among the islands of the group than the above meager notices would seem to indicate. Very little work has been done as yet in the waters surrounding the islands, even inshore, and their thorough examination will yield many facts of interest.

The natives report a small petrel, which they call by the above name, as common on the fishing grounds five or ten miles off the windward coast of Hawaii, and I have little doubt that it is this species, although I have not yet been able to obtain a specimen.

Description.—Adult. General color fuliginous; head and upper parts more slaty; remiges and rectrices dull black, the latter (except middle pair) white at base; upper tail-coverts white. Length about 8 inches.

Oceanodroma fuliginosa (Gmelin). Sooty Petrel.

According to Rothschild evidence of the occurrence of this petrel on Laysan was obtained by Prof. Schauinsland and later was verified by the finding of the species breeding in small numbers. The bird is chiefly known from the Japanese seas.

Description.—Adult. Crown, occiput, hind neck, scapulars and upper rump uniform dark sooty slate, darker and more sooty on posterior scapulars; lesser and uppermost median and greater wing-coverts sooty black; rest of wing-coverts and tertials light grayish brown; alula, primary coverts and remiges uniform sooty black; lower rump light grayish brown; upper tail-coverts and tail sooty black; anterior portion of head grayish brown; under parts sooty grayish brown. Length about 10 inches. (After Ridgway.)

Bulweria bulweri (Jard & Selby). Bulwer's Petrel.

Until somewhat recently this petrel was supposed to be wholly confined to the Atlantic Ocean where it has a wide range. The bird, however, was found by Mr. Palmer breeding commonly on French Frigate and also on Laysan Island. In the archipelago proper this petrel is known only from Kauai, where Mr. Knudsen collected two specimens.

Description.—Adult. Entire plumage sooty brownish black; bill black; feet brown. Length about 11½ inches.

Æstrelata phaeopygia sandwichensis (Ridgway). Uuau.

A female of this petrel in the juvenile plumage came ashore

on Hilo beach November 20, 1890, in an exhausted condition, and was secured by some boys by whom it was given to Mr. Newell, after having been kept alive for several days, when it died.

The natives inform me that the uuau is common on the fishing grounds, some five to ten miles off the windward side of Hawaii. They say also that formerly this bird nested in great numbers in the lava between Mauna Kea and Mauna Loa. They have visited the old nesting sites within a year or two, but report that they are no longer occupied, having been invaded by the mongoose.

It is said that years ago the nestlings of the uuau were considered a great delicacy, and were tabooed for the exclusive use of the chiefs. Natives were dispatched each season to gather the young birds which they did by inserting into the burrows a long stick and twisting it into the down of the young which then were easily pulled to the surface.

The native name for this bird, it is said, can be pronounced so as to exactly imitate its nocturnal cry.

The author feels reasonably sure that this species of petrel is the mysterious nightly visitor that for many years past has periodically invaded the town of Hilo upon dark and stormy nights, usually during the fall and winter months. The flying visits of the birds usually begin about half past seven or eight and, if the night be a stormy one with heavy showers of rain, the harsh, snarling cries of the bird may be heard intermittently all night long, as they fly rapidly back and forth over the zone of light that marks the populous part of the town. Whenever the heavy tropical showers cease, the cries are stilled, and the birds apparently retire to the sea; but the onset of another gust with accompanying rain is the signal for the return of the birds.

It is not surprising that these invisible visitors of the darkness, whose uncanny wailings come from the upper air, have excited the superstitious fears of the natives, and that they should interpret their voices as the sign of some unusual and calamitous event.

Upon a few occasions when the rain has been resolved into a fine mist and the electric light has been reflected upward as against a curtain, the writer has succeeded in getting a glimpse of the flying birds. Their white underparts, which can be plainly seen, and the peculiar character of their flight convince him beyond much doubt that the bird is none other than one of the petrels.

The birds fly a hundred yards and more above the earth, clearing the tops of the tallest palms, and the height has so far rendered futile all attempts to secure a specimen. Some of the natives solemnly declare, with a significant shake of the head, that they do not know the bird at all, that it has no name and has never been seen by human eye. Others, better informed or less superstitious, affirm with much positiveness that the bird is none other than the uuau; others believe it to be the ao; while others still are equally positive that it is the koae. The question can be settled absolutely only by obtaining a specimen—no easy task.

Description.—Adult. Above brownish slate, darker on wings and tail; head black; feathers of hind neck and upper tail-coverts white beneath the surface; forehead, lores, cheeks and under parts white; sides and flanks lightly barred (or not) with dusky; bill black; tarsus and upper half of foot flesh color; lower half of toes black. Wing, 10.75-11 inches; bill, about 1.20 inches.

Æstrelata hypoleuca, Salvin. Salvin's White-breasted Petrel.

"Palmer met with this rare petrel only on Laysan, where he found four moulting specimens in the daytime in deep burrows. They were completely dazed when taken out of their hiding places, and behaved as if they were quite blind. According to Mr. Freeth, their breeding-season was now over, June 16-26, but they came ashore in large numbers earlier during their breeding-time. They are quite nocturnal like other species of this genus."

Description.—Adult. Feathers of the forehead up to the middle of the head deep slate-color, broadly margined with white, and white at base; feathers just above the bill, lores, and entire under surface white; occiput and hind neck deep slate-color; feathers of the inter-scapular region back, and upper part of rump slate-color, with pale cinereous margins; lower rump deep slaty. * * * Length about 13 inches. (Rothschild.)

DIOMEDEIDAE. ALBATROSS FAMILY.

Diomedea immutabilis, Rothschild. White Albatross.

This albatross breeds in immense numbers upon Laysan and also upon Lisiansky islands. Apparently it is more or less common throughout the Hawaiian main group, though it is not known to breed upon any of them.

Description.—Adult. "Head, neck, lower rump, and entire under surface pure white; space in front of the eye sooty black; wings and wing-coverts blackish brown; interscapular region, back, and upper part of rump paler and more smoky brown; tail black, fading into white at base; under wing-coverts mixed blackish brown and white. Total length about 32 inches." (Rothschild.)

Diomedea nigripes, Aud. Brown Gooney.

This is the gooney that follows in the wake of ships from San Francisco to Honolulu and Hilo. The birds feed upon the scraps of pork and meat thrown overboard from the kitchen, and it is simply amazing that birds will fly so far and take so much trouble for such meager reward. Usually the last gooney parts company with the southward bound ship when some 500 miles off the islands, but occasionally individuals keep on till immediately off the harbors. At rare intervals I hear of an albatross coming ashore on Hawaii to roost for an hour or so on the rocks, but whether this or the preceding species cannot be determined as no specimens have been collected.

Description.—Adult. Dusky throughout; grayer beneath; forehead, tail-coverts and base of tail white. Length 28.50-36.00 inches.

LARIDÆ. GULL AND TERN FAMILY.

Sterna fuliginosa, Gmelin. Ewaena; Sooty Tern.

I have not found this tern upon the coast of the island of Hawaii although it may occur there in small numbers as it has been taken upon the shores of Oahu and Kauai, and Mr. Palmer found it breeding abundantly upon Laysan island.

Description.—Adult. Upper parts sooty black; forehead, sides of head, and under parts white, as also mostly the outer pair of tail-feathers; bill and feet black. Length about 15-17 inches.

Sterna lunata, Peale. Pakalakala. Bridled Tern.

This is another species of tern which has not yet been found on the coast of the island of Hawaii, the shores of this island being perhaps less adapted to the habits of the gulls and terns than those of any other of the group. It was found, however, upon Kauai by Mr. Knudsen, and Palmer found it in abundance upon Laysan. The bird deposits but one egg, and this on the sand.

Description.—Adult. Upper parts dark ashy, paler on the hind neck; forehead, a broad stripe through the eye and entire under parts white; head and neck black. Outer webs of primaries blackish; inner webs white with a black stripe along the shaft. Outer webs of tail-feathers gray, inner webs white; outer pair of rectrices white. Length about 16.50 inches.

Sterna paradisæa Brunn. Arctic Tern.

The only claim this tern has to recognition here is the occurrence of a lone individual on Hilo beach May 9, 1891. The bird boarded a schooner bound for Hilo when four days off port, but disappeared on the third day following, having evidently sighted land. It was next seen on the beach by some boys, and was in such an exhausted condition that it was caught by hand, and, still living, came into the possession of Mr. R. T. Guard. It died the following day, probably from exhaustion and starvation, as it was much emaciated, and subsequently was kindly presented to the writer.

Presumably the bird was migrating somewhere along the American coast towards Alaska when, in some way, it was lost or blown out to sea, and made the weary passage nearly to Hawaii, probably with neither rest nor food.

Description.—Adult. Top of head black; above deep pearl-gray; tips of secondaries, rump, upper tail-coverts and tail white; beneath deep lavender gray; sides of head and lower tail-coverts white; outer web of outer tail feather dusky; bill and feet carmine; length 14 to 17 inches. In winter the crown is white with black streaks; the lower parts white.

Sterna melanauchen Temm.

Two specimens are reported by Mr. Bryan to be in the Bishop Museum which were taken at Mana on the island of Kauai by Mr. A. F. Judd during the winter of 1892-93. "Both have the white foreheads assumed by this species, while the remainder of the plumage is badly worn."

December 24, 1901, a third specimen of this tern was obtained at Hakalau by Mr. H. Beveridge during a severe and prolonged storm. The bird evidently was a wanderer and had left the sea to seek shelter on the land. It is in excellent plumage. The bill of this specimen is black, the extreme tip lighter. The legs and ·feet in life were orange, or perhaps red. Mr. Bryan has kindly compared this bird with the museum specimens and his remarks are added. "The Museum specimens are much more badly worn. The bills are *horn* black, with lighter tip; the feet indicate red, though very much discolored. The black patch in front of eye is better defined in your specimen, and the Museum specimens have more dark feathers about the carpal joint. I should judge your bird to be adult while ours are more immature."

The tern is of far southern distribution in the Pacific, occurring through Polynesia generally, the Philippines and on the Chinese coast. It is probably entirely accidental in the Hawaiian Islands.

Description.—Adult. "Crown always white, sometimes with a brownish tinge; nape, orbit, and ear coverts black; mantle pale gray; in front of the eye a black triangular patch, the point of which does not reach to the base of the bill; from the eyes a black band extending about the back of the head; band broadened and more or less prolonged down the back of the neck; neck and under parts white; mantle and rump pearl gray; shafts of the primaries white; outer primary with the outer web blackish. streak next the shaft on the inner web blackish or grayish black." Length about 13.25-13.50. (Bryan.)

Anous stolidus (Linnaeus). Noddy Tern.

This tern was found by Palmer breeding upon French Frigate and Laysan Islands, and hence may be expected to occur as a visitor on the Hawaiian group from where, however, no present record of it exists.

Description.—Adult. Sooty brown, grayer on neck and passing into white on forehead; quills nearly black. Length 13.00-16.75.

Anous hawaiiensis, Rothschild. Noio.

This tern was well named *hawaiiensis*, for it may be regarded as *the* Hawaiian tern. It is found in colonies all along the coast of the island of Hawaii, wherever caves and ledges occur in the face of the cliffs suitable for roosting places and for nesting sites. It probably occurs, also, on all the other islands. The noio lives wholly upon fish, to obtain which it habitually makes excursions off shore ten or fifteen miles. Indeed comparatively little of its food is obtained in shore, though occasionally the birds may be seen slowly winnowing their way along the surf-streaked coast, and scanning the heaving billows with anxious eye for their quarry.

While following its prey on the broad ocean the noio is of much service to the Hawaiian fishermen, and acts as his pilot; for its presence in numbers in a given spot marks the whereabouts of shoals of noi, a long silvery minnow, and there also is sure to be found the aku, or skipjack, much sought after by the fishermen.

This tern never dives for fish but with a quick stoop and a dip of the head it seizes the unsuspecting minnow when close to the surface.

In the olden time I learn that the natives used to raid the nesting sites of the noio pretty regularly for both eggs and young, the latter especially being esteemed delicacies as indeed were the young of most sea-birds. For this purpose dark nights were usually chosen and by means of torches and the help of clubs the old birds, bewildered by the light, were easily secured.

A few straws picked up from the surface of the sea—a mere apology for a nest—serves to keep the one egg from rolling off the ledge. The egg is very large for the size of the bird, and the ground color is light buff spotted heavily with dark brown and purplish.

Description.—Adult. Forehead and top of head ashy white, gradually merging into sooty black of back; hind neck and upper part of back ashy

gray; wings sooty black; tail grayish; beneath sooty black. Length about
13.50 inches.

Gygis alba (Sparrman).   White Tern.

Included by Mr. Dole in his list of 1869 and found by Palmer
breeding upon Laysan and Lisiansky Islands. Doubtless this tern
will be found to occur upon the Hawaiian group, at least upon
the northern members, as an occasional visitor.

Description.—Adult. White, eye encircled narrowly with black. Bill
and feet black. Length about 13 inches.

Larus barrovianus Ridgway.   Point Barrow Gull.

Mr. Bryan reports (Key to the Birds of the Hawaiian Group)
two specimens of this gull as having been taken on the island of
Kauai by Mr. Francis Gay and a third as being in the Museum of
St. Louis College. The latter was procured on the island of Maui
by Brother Matthias. These birds would seem to be accidental
strays from the Alaskan coast.

Description.—Adult. Head, neck, tail and under parts white; mantle
pale pearl gray.
In winter, head and neck streaked with brownish. Length about 25-28
inches.

Larus glaucescens, Naum.   Glaucous-winged Gull.

This gull seems to be a rare and irregular visitor to the island
of Hawaii and probably also to the other islands, especially to
Oahu. Every year or two, one or more individuals are seen about
Hilo harbor, evidently having followed vessels down from San
Francisco. Apparently these wanderers never attempt to return,
but their final fate is unknown.

According to Rothschild, Prof. Schauinsland obtained a specimen of this species on Laysan.

Description.—Adult. Mantle pearl gray; head and under parts white;
primaries with small white spots at the tips; in winter top of head and
hind neck streaked with dusky. Length about 25 inches. The young
are gray more or less variegated with white.

Larus philadelphia (Ord). Bonaparte's Gull.

Rothschild records the fact that a young female of this species was obtained by Palmer at Poli-hule lake on Kauai, March 15, 1891. So far as known at present this is the first and only record of the bird in the islands.

Description.—Adult. Head plumbeous; mantle pearl gray; under parts white; feet orange red. Adult in winter has a white head and flesh colored feet. Length from 12-14 inches.

Larus franklinii Sw. & Rich. Franklin's Rosy Gull.

Mr. Bryan reports a single specimen of this species as having been taken on the island of Maui by Brother Matthias. The specimen is now in the St. Louis College cabinet. As this gull is an inhabitant of the interior of the American continent the presence on the islands even of a single individual must be regarded as very remarkable.

Description.—Adult. Head black, with white on eyelid; mantle plumbeus; quills bluish gray, white tipped. In winter similar, but head white. Length about 13.50-15 inches.

Larus delawarensis Ord. Ring-billed Gull.

Mr. Bryan reports a single specimen of this gull as being in the St. Louis College cabinet from the "Hawaiian Islands." Like several other of the American coast gulls its presence in the Hawaiian Islands is accidental. In time, no doubt, all of the northwest coast gulls will in like manner appear as casual visitors.

Description.—Adult. Mantle pearl gray; lower parts, white; bill greenish yellow, black banded near tip. Length about 18-20 inches.

Larus californicus Lawr. California Gull.

A specimen of this gull is reported by Mr. Bryan to be in the St. Louis College cabinet from the "Hawaiian Islands." Its presence here, like that of the preceding species, is, of course, purely accidental.

Description.—Adult. Mantle dark gray; bill yellow with a crimson spot near end of lower mandible; scapulars and secondaries broadly tipped with white. In winter, head and neck broadly streaked with brown. Length about 20-23 inches.

LIST OF BIRDS INTRODUCED INTO THE ISLANDS.

For the sake of completeness a list of the birds that have been purposely introduced into one or more of the islands of the group, and that have become established, is appended. For remarks upon this subject more in extenso the reader is referred to a paper by the author in the Hawaiian Annual for 1900.

PLOCEIDÆ. WEAVER BIRD FAMILY.

Munia nisoria punctata (Temm.). Rice Bird.

Originally introduced from the Malayan Peninsula into Oahu, but now apparently distributed over all the islands of the group and abundant in most localities. Where there are no rice fields the bird is harmless enough, but it is a nuisance in the rice patches and the cause of much loss to the planter.

Description.—Adult. Above chocolate brown; shafts of feathers white; throat deep chestnut; sides of body streaked. Length about 4.50.

FRINGILLIDÆ. FINCH AND SPARROW FAMILY.

Passer domesticus Linn. European House Finch.

Apparently this undesirable little pest (little in size but great in its capacity for mischief) is chiefly, if not wholly, confined to the island of Oahu, where it was first introduced. It is abundant about Honolulu. By determined and sustained effort it would be possible to exterminate the species in Oahu before it has secured a foothold in the other islands, and so to eliminate it as a certain source of danger to the agriculturalist. The history of this finch in America and the extent of the damage it inflicts are too well known to need repetition here.

Description.—Adult male. Above brown, back streaked with black;

wing twice banded with white; throat blackhead grayish with patch of chestnut; under parts grayish. Female duller. Length 5.50-6.25.

Carpodacus mexicanus frontalis (Say). Crimson-headed Finch. "Linnet."

This pretty finch is probably established on all the islands. Upon certain parts of the islands of Hawaii and Maui it is exceedingly numerous and is increasing all the time. The windward and rainy regions are not well suited to its habits, but in dry climates as in Kau, Hawaii, and in some districts of Maui the bird flourishes remarkably and may there be seen in large flocks. Were it not for its fruit-eating proclivities, the trim form and pleasant song of this finch would make it a welcome addition to the island avifauna.

Description.—Adult male. Above ashy brown, streaked with darker; forehead lores, throat, breast and rump crimson; sides much streaked with brown; abdomen ashy. Female duller. Length about 5.50.

STURNIDÆ. STARLING FAMILY.

Acridotheres tristis (Linn.). Mynah.

The mynah, originally a native of India, is now widespread over the islands, and there is no doubt that the bird is constantly increasing in numbers. Notwithstanding that the mynah destroys vast numbers of insects and in this way is of direct and great value in the cane-fields, in the pastures and among horses and cattle, there is a strong and growing prejudice in the islands against the bird.

The charge is made that the mynah invades the cote of the domestic pigeon, and even ejects the eggs and young birds. That the mynah sometimes dispossess the pigeon of its home there is no doubt, although, on the other hand, it not rarely shares a portion of the cote with the proper owners, and seems to rear its young on not unfriendly terms with them. The object of the mynah is not direct injury to the pigeons—for apparently it eats neither their eggs nor their young—but is solely to find a safe

9-H B

place for their own eggs, the mynah being partial to boxes and to cavities in trees in which to nest.

In any event little damage is to be apprehended from the above source, since the cote can be freed from mynahs with but little trouble. A much more serious charge against the mynah is that it has a strong partiality for figs and other small fruits. The bird is and always will be a nuisance to the fruit grower.

There is still another and even more serious charge made against the mynah, viz.: that it destroys and drives away the native birds. It is an undoubted fact that practically all native Hawaiian birds are diminishing in numbers, and the belief is widespread that the mynah is directly responsible for the dimunition.

Thus Mr. Rothschild in Vol. iii of the Avifauna of Laysan, p. 300, states that the mynah "kills and eats the young and eggs of small birds." Unfortunately this author gives no specific cases, and does not mention the birds attacked. Probably, however, native birds are the ones in mind.

More recently still Mr. Perkins (Ibis for October, 1901) affirms that the mynah "not only attacks and drives away other birds, but also devours their eggs and young." He adds further (p. 580) that he has himself seen the mynah "devouring both young and eggs of other species." Such evidence is of course conclusive enough, although, again, it is unfortunate that more specific information is not given.

Of course if the destruction of eggs and of the young of smaller species is a general and confirmed habit of the mynah, inquirers need seek no further for the cause of the recent decrease in the number of native birds, and the mynah should be condemned to immediate extermination if that be possible. I believe, however, the above observations to be highly exceptional, and that such acts of the mynah are very rare.

I have had the mynah under observation in town, in pasture land and in the forest for several years, having early surmised that the bird might ultimately prove injurious to the native species, and I have never seen a mynah attack or in any way disturb a native bird, though hundreds of times I have observed the small native species feeding in the same trees with mynahs, neither paying the slightest attention to the other. Nor has diligent inquiry among the natives and settlers revealed anyone else who has seen the mynah exhibit signs of hostility towards the native birds.

If any of the native birds nested in the cavities of trees, there is not the slightest doubt that they would be dispossessed by the mynah. Or if there was a conflict over food, the native birds would soon be driven to the wall by the larger and fiercer mynah. The food habits of the mynah seem, however, to conflict very little, if any, with the native species.

Even a species which is in the main beneficial may increase to such an extent as to be a nuisance, and such seems likely to be the case with the mynah. Its numbers, even at present, are startling, and there seems to be no limit to the possibilities of its increase. Any altitude, high or low, is suited to its tastes. It is true that the bird shuns the denser forest, but in tracts where the undergrowth has been somewhat thinned by cattle it is entirely at home, no matter how far from civilization.

It is distinctly possible that it is to the immense numbers of the mynah, which sometimes seem to fill the forest trees with their flocks, and to their harsh noises, rather to any direct hostility or injury by them, that is due the antipathy of native birds, if such they have. So far as my own observations go I am bound to state, as above, that I have never noted such antipathy. Perhaps the native birds passively endure the hated presence of the noisy strangers till they finally abandon a locality in sheer disgust.

All theories aside, the important fact is that the mynah was introduced into the Hawaiian Islands, unadvisedly as most think, that the bird has increased to an amazing extent and is still increasing without sign of abatement. I have endeavored to take as optimistic a view of its presence in the Islands as possible, for, apparently, the bird is here to stay. For the mynah is a wary bird, and neither the gun, traps or poison are likely ever to have any serious effect upon its numbers. The further increase of the bird may, perhaps, be checked, though not without much expense, but its extermination is practically impossible.

The lesson of its introduction into the Islands is an easy one to read, and should be profited by.

Description.—Adult. Above brown, as also breast and sides; head and neck blackish; a bare patch of yellow behind eye; wing barred with white; abdomen and under tail-coverts white; bill yellow. Length about 9.50.

ALAUDIDÆ. LARK FAMILY.

Alauda arvensis Linn. Skylark.

The European skylark was introduced into Oahu several years since, and the experiment appears to have been a great success.* The bird is now found in several parts of the island and seems to be constantly increasing in numbers, though not very rapidly. I believe that the bird is found in small numbers upon Maui. A few have been brought from Oahu to the windward side of Hawaii, but their fate is at present unknown.

Description.—Adult. General color brown streaked with black; chest buffy, black streaked; outer tail-feathers nearly all white. Length about 7.50.

PSITTACIDÆ. PARROT FAMILY.

Platycercus palliceps. Blue-cheeked Parrot.

The presence of this parrot in a wild state was detected by Palmer in 1892 on Haleakala, Maui, and several specimens were secured. In June of 1901 the writer found the bird to be by no means uncommon in the forest on the slopes of Haleakala at an

---

*The introduction of the skylark into these islands is to be credited to Hon. A. S. Cleghorn, who imported them from New Zealand in the latter part of the year 1870. This initial lot was turned over to Judge Robt. Moffitt, of Kahuku, Oahu, who liberated them on the high table land of Leilehua and open mountain slopes. A subsequent colony from and through the same source was given to the late Albert Jaeger, who set them free at Moiliili, or upper Waikiki.

altitude of about 6,000 feet. This locality, above Olinda, was somewhere near the place where the bird was found by Palmer.

Those seen by me were mostly in pairs and probably were nesting, so that I did not molest them. They were usually feeding upon grass seeds on the edges of the forest, and when alarmed immediately took refuge in its depths. Mr. H. P. Baldwin has a small patch of corn at Olinda, and I was told that when this was in the ear the parrots visited the patch in great numbers to feed upon the ripening ears.

With reference to the origin of these wild parrots, I am informed that they came from a pair which were liberated years ago at Ulupalakua, East Maui, by Captain Makee. The pair remained near the premises for a long time, until in fact they had reared a young one, when they left.

This parrot is a native of eastern Australia.

Description.—Adult. Head pale yellow; cheeks white, bordered below with blue; feathers of the nape, back and scapulars black, broadly margined with gamboge-yellow; rump feathers and upper tail-coverts very pale greenish blue with the bases black; under surface bluish, each feather fringed with black; under tail-coverts scarlet; wings blue. Length about 13 inches. (Salvadori.)

COLUMBIDÆ. DOVE AND PIGEON FAMILY.

Turtur chinensis (Scop.). ' Chinese Turtle Dove.

Introduced a number of years ago and now more or less abundant on all the islands. This dove is partial to a dry climate, and hence does not thrive and multiply on the windward side of Hawaii and the other islands as it does in the less rainy sections. In some localities doves are exceedingly numerous, and are much sought after by sportsmen. They are found in the mountains to an altitude of at least 6,000 feet.

Description.—Adult. Upper parts generally light brown; hind neck black with white spotting; occiput bluish gray; outer tail-feathers broadly tipped with white. Length 12-13 inches.

Lophortyx californicus (Shaw).   California Valley Quail.

Introduced many years ago and formerly abundant on all the islands. In most regions the bird has been practically exterminated from the lowlands but in certain localities, as upon Hawaii, is still abundant in the regions above heavy timber, at an elevation of 6,000 or 7,000 feet, where the mongoose, its deadly enemy, has but a slight foothold.

Description.—Adult male. Above brownish ash; occiput brown; crest black; throat black, bordered by white line; breast slaty blue; belly chestnut, with scale-like markings. Female smaller and duller. Length about 11 inches.

PHASIANIDÆ.   PHEASANT FAMILY.

Phasianus torquatus Gmel.   Mongolian Pheasant.

Introduced from China several years ago and now well established on Oahu, Molokai and Kauai.

Description.—Adult male. Upper parts chestnut; a white ring around the metallic green neck; breast with metallic reflections. Female duller and smaller. Length 20 to 30 inches.

Phasianellus versicolor Vieill.   Japanese Pheasant.

Occupies about the same status in the islands as the preceding species.

Description.—Adult. General color dark green, lower neck and mantle variegated with buff; no white nuchal ring. Female duller and blacker. Length 24-29 inches.

RALLIDÆ.   RAIL GALLINULE FAMILY.

Porphyrio melanotus Newton.   Alae awi.

This Gallinule seems to be rather numerous in the taro patches and rice swamps of Oahu, having been introduced from Australia. So far as I am informed it has not reached the other islands.

Description.—Adult.   Above black; below bluish; thighs purplish brown; under tail-coverts white; bill, frontal plate, legs and feet red. Length about 17.25.

Many years ago the domestic fowl took to the forests and soon became as wild there, and in as complete a state of nature, as before it was domesticated.   In a similar way, though perhaps not quite to the same extent, the turkey returned to its natural wild state, and in many regions became abundant.   Both species furnished excellent sport, and supplied welcome tidbits for the table. The introduction of the mongoose changed all this, and today both birds have been practically exterminated by that animal, assisted, no doubt, by wild cats and wild dogs, both the latter being numerous in some regions.

TABLE SHOWING THE DISTRIBUTION OF BIRDS (OTHER THAN INTRODUCED) BY ISLANDS.

NAME. X indicates a resident species: O extinct species; † migrate and accidental.	HAWAII	MAUI	LANAI	MOLOKAI	OAHU	KAUAI	NIIHAU	Læ; san or the other "Bird Isls"
Phæornis obscura, Omao	X							
oahensis, Oahu Omao					O			
myadestina, Kamao						X		
palmeri, Puaiohi						X		
lanaiensis, Oloma'o			X					
Acrocephalus familiaris, Miller Bird								X
Chasiempis sandwichensis, Elepaio	X							
ridgwayi*, Chestnut colored Elepaio	X							
gayi, Oahu Elepaio					X			
schlateri, Kauai Elepaio						X		
Corvus tropicus, Alala	X							
Hemignathus obscurus, Akialoa	X							
procerus, Iiwi						X		
lanaiensis, Lanai Akialoa			X					
ellisianus, Oahu Akialoa					O			
Heterorynchus wilsoni, Akipolaau	X							
lucidus, Oahu Akipolaau					O			
affinis, Maui Akipolaau		X						
hanapepe, Nukupuu						X		
Viridonia sagittirostris, Green Solitaire	X							....
Chlorodrepanis virens, Hawaii Amakihi	X							
wilsoni, Maui Amakihi		X						
chloris, Oahu Amakihi					X			
stejnegeri, Stejneger's Amakihi						X		
parva, Alawi						X		
Oreomyza mana, Olive Green Creeper	X							
perkinsi, Perkin's Creeper	X							
bairdi, Akikiki						X		
flammea, Kakawahie				X				
newtoni, Maui Creeper		X						
maculata, Oahu Creeper					X			
montana, Alauhiio			X					
Drepanis pacifica, Mamo	O							
funerea, Black Mamo				O				
Vestiaria cocinea, Iiwi	X	X	X	X	X	X		
Palmeria dolei, Crested Honey Eater		X						
Himatione sanguinea, Akakani	X	X	X	X	X	X		
fraithii, Laysan Akakani								X
Ciridops anna, Ulaaihawane	O							
Loxops coccinea, Akepeuie	X							

*This form does not appear in the previous list. It is the Elepaio occupying much of the windward side of Hawaii, there replacing *sandwichensis* which is confined to the leeward side of the island. Ridgwayi is more deeply colored, and the white markings of *sandwichensis* are mostly replaced by chestnut.

TABLE SHOWING THE DISTRIBUTION OF BIRDS (OTHER THAN INTRODUCED) BY ISLANDS.

NAME.	HAWAII	MAUI	LANAI	MOLOKAI	OAHU	KAUAI	NIIHAU	LAYSAN OR THE OTHER "BIRD ISLS"
Loxops rufa, Oahu Akepeuie					O			
ochracea, Ochraceous Akepeuie..		X						
caeruleirostris, Ou-holowai....						X		
Pseudonestor xanthophrys, Parrot-billed Koa Finch............		X						
Psittirostra psittacea, Ou.....	X	X	X	X		X		
olivacea, Oahu Ou..........					O ?			
Loxioides bailleui, Palila...	X							
Telespiza cantans, Laysan Finch..,								X
Rhodacanthis palmeri, Hopue; Orange Koa Finch............	X							
flaviceps, Yellow-headed Koa Finch......................	X							
Chloridops kona, Palila..........	X							
Moho nobilis, O-o..	X							
apicalis, Oahu O-o.....					O			
bishopi, Molokai O-o				X				
braccatus, O-o A-a..............						X		
Chætoptila angustipluma.........	O							
Caryle alcyon............	†							
Buteo solitarius, Io......	X							
Circus hudsonius, Marsh Hawk. ..						†		
Pandion haliæstus carolinensis, American Osprey............						†		
Asio accipitrinus sandwichensis, Pueo.....................	X	X	X	X	X	X	X	
Strepsilas interpres, Akekeke	X	X		X	X	X		
Charadrius squatarola, Black-bellied Plover..............	†							
dominicus fulvus, Kolea.........	†	†	†	†	†	†	†	
Numenius tahitiensis, Kioea.......	†	†		†	†	†	†	
Heteractitis incanus, Ulili....	†	†	†	†	†	†	X	†
Limosa lapponica baueri, Pacific Godwit......................		†				†		†
Calidris arenaria, Hunakai........	†	†		†	†	†		
Tringa acuminata, Sharp-tailed Sandpiper..................		†				†		†
Tringa maculata, Pectoral Sandpiper......................	†							
Gallinago delicata, Wilson's Snipe.	†							
Himantopus knudseni, Kukuluaeo..		X		X	X			
Crymophilus fulicarius, Red Phalarope...................	†	†						

TABLE SHOWING THE DISTRIBUTION OF BIRDS (OTHER THAN INTRODUCED) BY ISLANDS.

NAME.	HAWAII	MAUI	LANAI	MOLOKAI	OAHU	KAUAI	NIIHAU	LAYSAN OR THE OTHER "BIRD ISLS"
Crymophilus lobatus Northern, Phalarope	†							---
Pennula millsi, Moho	O							...-
sandwichensis.,	O							
Porzanula palmeri, Laysan Crake..								X
Fulica alai, Alae Keokeo	X	X			X	X		....
Gallinula galeata sandwichensis, Alae Ula	X	X		X	X		X	....
Ardea sacra, Aukuu	†	†						...
Nycticorax nycticorax griseus, Aukuu Kahili	X	X	X	X	X	X		....
Plegadis guarauna, Glossy Ibis				X		X		
Bernicla sandwichensis, Nene	X	O						
Branta nigricans, Black Brant		†						
canadensis minima, Cackling Goose	†					†		....
Chen hyperborea, Lesser Snow Goose		†						†
Anser albifrons gambeli, White-fronted Goose	†							
Dafila acuta, Pintail	†	†		†	†	†	....	
Spatula clypeata, Koloa Moha	†	†		†	†			
Anas americana, Baldpate								†
boschas, Mallard								†
carolinensis, Green-winged Teal								†
wyvilliana, Koloa	X	X			X	X		....
laysanensis, Laysan Teal								X
Mergus serrator, Red-breasted Merganser	†			†				---
Charitonetta albeola, Buffle-head		†						†
Fregata aquila, Iwa		†	†	†	†	†	†	†
Phacrocorax pelagicus, Pelagic Cormorant	†?							†
Sula cyanops, Masked Gannet								†
piscator, Red-footed Booby					†		†	†
sula, Booby								†
Phæthon. lepturus Koae	X	X	X	X	X	X		...
rubricauda, Red-tailed Koae	†					X	X	X
Puffinus cuneatus, Wedge-tailed Puffin						X		X
newelli, Newell's Puffin		X				X		......
nativitatis, Christmas Island Shearwater								X
Oceanodroma castro, Ake Ake	X?					X		X
fuliginosa, Sooty Petrel								X
Bulweria bulweri, Bulwer's Petrel	X					X		X

TABLE SHOWING THE DISTRIBUTION OF BIRDS (OTHER THAN INTRODUCED) BY ISLANDS.

NAME.	Hawaii	Maui	Lanai	Molokai	Oahu	Kauai	Niihau	Layson or the other "Bird Isls"
Aestrelata phæopygia sandwichensis, Uuau..	X					X		X
hypoleuca, Salvin's White-breasted Petrel..								†
Diomedie immutabilis, White Albatros							X	X
nigripes, Brown Gooney	†					†	†	X
Sterna fuliginosa, Ewaena					X	X		X
lunata, Pakalakala								X
paradisea, Arctic Tern	†							
Sterna melanauchen	†					†		
Anous stolidus, Noddy Tern	†			X	X	X		X
hawaiiænsis, Noio	X			X	X	X	X	X
Gygis alba, White Tern								X
Larus barrovianus, Point Barrow Gull	†	†				†		†
glaucescens, Glaucous-winged Gull	†							†
philadelphia, Bonaparte's Gull						†		..
franklinii, Franklin's Rosy Gull								..
delawarensis, Ring-billed Gull		†		†				..
californicus, California Gull		†						..

The above list contains 125 species, including residents, migrants and strays, together with a few that are extinct or practically so. 11 additional species have been introduced into one or more islands, and now are more or less firmly established. There are 60 species of woodland Passeres that are endemic and are peculiar to the islands, these being distinctively *the* Hawaiian Birds.

INDEX.

About the author

Henry Wetherbee Henshaw was born in Cambridgeport, Massachusetts in 1850. Early training in biology and ornithology later led to a highly successful career in the developing field of anthropology. From 1872 to 1879, Henshaw was a naturalist and ornithologist with the Wheeler Survey for Exploration of the West, and from 1879 to 1893 worked at the US Bureau of Ethnology. At the Bureau, Henshaw worked on the classification of native North American languages using a biological model of groupings by stock. In addition to this work, he prepared a map of tribal territories at the time of contact, as well as other researches into the original native tribes. His contributions were important to the creation of the Handbook of American Indians North of Mexico

In 1885 the British Museum acquired his collection of birds. From 1889 to 1893, he was Editor of "American Anthropologist." In 1893, Henshaw collected the holotype of Xantusia henshawi, at Witch Creek, San Diego County, California.

From 1894 to 1904 health reasons sent Henshaw on a ten year sabbatical to the Hawaiian Islands. There he practiced photography and wrote *Birds of the Hawaiian Islands* (1902). From 1905 through 1916, he was appointed Administrative Assistant, Bureau of Biological Survey, US Department of Agriculture and from 1910 on was the Chief of the US Biological Survey. Declining health forced his resignation in 1916. He died in Washington, DC in 1930.